ROAD SAFETY

ROAD SAFETY

HOW TO REDUCE ROAD ACCIDENTS

by

T. S. SKILLMAN

M. A. (Cantab.), M. I. E. E.

THE RE-APPRAISAL SOCIETY

Distributed in U.S.A. by

DAVID McKAY COMPANY, INC.
NEW YORK

To
JOE O'LEARY
of Elizabeth, New Jersey

The Re-Appraisal Society is a new organization. Its addresses are:—

England: 29 Old Bond Street, London, W.1.

U.S.A.: 4063 Radford Avenue, Studio City, California 91604

Australia: 136 Milson Road, Cremorne, Sydney, N.S.W.

Objectives of the Re-Appraisal Society

To encourage thought and discussion throughout the community on the problems of our civilization by:

(1) The collection, systematization and distribution of factual data;

(2) the establishment of data centres for the use of members of the Society;

(3) the distribution to members of material to form a basis for discussion;

(4) the dissemination of the resultant knowledge and opinions via all available channels of communication;

(5) the establishment of a working relationship with all bodies concerned with these problems.

Contents

PART III: MISCELLANEOUS POINTS

Preface

CAN SOCIETY BEAT THE TRAFFIC PROBLEM?

We are told road accidents must always be with us; that driving is a complicated art, speeds are higher than those for which Nature designed us, and only a split second response can stand between us and disaster at any time. We are told the problem is a matter of minimizing the frequency of the accidents by careful training, and minimizing their magnitude by building safer cars and roads. So the cry goes, and to some degree it is true.

Yet the average man drives for thirty years per crash. Is he then slipping and slithering past disaster by a hair's breadth for all that long time? Does he go for hour after hour in mortal danger, and still escape for all those years?

No, indeed. He does take many chances – an average of about 70,000 per accident. But each of these persists for only a second or so, which represents in total only about 0.1% of his driving time. For the other 99.9% he is as safe, even on a high speed road or in dense traffic, as when he is strolling along the sidewalk.

He must look where he is going, and dodge the hazards. He was equipped to do this aeons ago, when his ancestors first learned to run. This is why he lasts these thirty years, not because of some strenuous anxious unflagging application of superhuman wariness and skill. No great strain is involved at all, unless he is scared. Scare him and it becomes a constant effort. He loses his God-given powers of automatic self protection.

The view advanced in this book is that it is well within the powers of nearly every unfrightened driver to reduce those 70,000 ' vulnerabilities ' to 7,000, which will increase his safe time to 99.99%, and virtually eliminate all accidents derived from careless driving (80% to 90% of the whole).

Will Society make a serious effort to bring this about? Also to eliminate the residual accidents such as those produced by mechanical failures? There is no sign yet that it will. No one believes it is possible, so no one tries.

This is a sad situation. Traffic accidents are a source of atrocious waste and vast distress. We *must* eliminate them.

The blocking factor in this, as in many other social difficulties, is our inability to reach the mind of the ordinary man. He avoids the effort of thought. Serious discussion is quickly broken up by some hearty or facetious remark. It is fashionable to do this and much admired. Anyone who feels otherwise is a bore and loses status. We have no longer any communication channel which will carry difficult or complex ideas to the general public. Everything must be simplified and pre-digested. ' Tell me the gist of it in two sentences ' is the cry, even in the board room. The resultant oversimplification is often hopelessly inadequate or misleading.

This, it is said, is human nature. It may be within everyone's power to drive safely, but few people want to. There is no adequate motivation. This is not peculiar to motoring. It is a basic characteristic of our society in its attitude to most social troubles. We read but we don't think. As a community, we swallow ideas whole, like a hungry dog, or reject them angrily if they aren't immediately acceptable. No writer or broadcaster who ignores this will long survive.

We seem to be less wise even than we were centuries ago. It was once generally held that teaching people to read would open their minds. It seems to have had the opposite effect – to have made them more vulnerable to specious nonsense, to demagoguery, to the charms of the sneer technique, and the comforting alibis of degeneracy. Or perhaps we have given a voice to poorer quality minds who years ago would have been inarticulate. Whatever the reasons, we seem stuck with a wide range of social problems, derived from poor thinking, and all reacting directly on to road accidents.

To break this, we need to change human nature. We must get the ordinary man to enjoy thinking.

The proposition is that human nature is only part animal inheritance. Much of it is tradition, habit, and fashion . . . all of which can be changed, *given time*. A fifty-year plan is called for, with the nice easy approach that is essential in the early stages of any marathon. This calls for an organization with a life longer than any individual, something that makes small demands on its participants, something easy and enjoyable, something not discouraged by apparent failure in the early stages, and satisfied with small yields. This organization has to be quite different from the ordinary earnest reform movement, where dedication and zeal are a virtue and where the leadership goes to those vital people who want to get something done and show results. It must be a slow, lazy affair, not in a hurry and not intending to make too much of itself. This is the Re-appraisal Society. It aims to start a new fashion or habit – that of thinking and talking about social problems.

Two hundred years ago if you had suggested that everyone could learn to read, you would have been greeted with ribald disbelief. Reading was something only the finest brains could aspire to. So it is today with thinking. ' What! ' they say, ' Get those dull, discouraged people or their grandsons to re-assess their values, to bring discipline to their daily life, discernment to mass propaganda, and discrimination to politics? Never! ' The Re-appraisal Society says otherwise. It can be done; in a hundred years; perhaps in fifty; perhaps even less because to some degree it is already on its way. The trend is discernible.

The Society plans to persuade ordinary people to take another look – a very hard look – not only at road accidents, but at the whole of our social set-up, personal, communal, racial and international. Are we getting the kind of homes and cities and schools and institutions that we really need? Do we treat criminals with wisdom? Are we defending ourselves adequately from malevolent and subversive activities? These questions and many more can have a profound effect on our personal happiness and the welfare of our children.

The easiest and most enjoyable way to think about a problem is to discuss it. It is also the most effective way. We are unlikely to change a man's views by lecturing him or exhorting him or trying to frighten him. But discussion makes him think. As one man put it, in another connection, ' I never intended to give up smoking. One day I got into an argument with a fellow who wanted to. He said it couldn't be done. I said it could. Now he still smokes, but I've given it up.'

The method which the Society follows is to distribute discussion sheets, of which a sample is given below, and data sheets. A member is asked only to glance at these and then file them away. Sooner or later – we are not in a hurry – something will catch his interest and he will want to play a more active part. He will start talking, and therefore thinking, about it. We are not primarily interested in what conclusions are reached, only in arriving at the point where he enjoys the discussions, and discovers that intelligent conversation can be just as much fun as the frivolous small talk which is at present so fashionable at all levels.

Our progress in early years will be small. Success depends on whether we can secure as members people of the kind that start a new fashion. This may take ten or twenty years, but once established any new fashion can be counted on to spread through the body of the community relatively quickly. It may seem at first sight a strange proposition that our members' success in staging a few enjoyable discussions with friends on road accidents and kindred problems can have the effect of eliminating road accidents; yet all the work that has been done on this seems to indicate not merely that it is a possible solution, but that it is the only first step which can be categorized as truly hard-headed.

These long-dated, mild, activities will not compete with any of the many specialist bodies already working on these different problems, road accidents or otherwise. The Re-Appraisal Society sees itself as no rival to any of these, but as a kind of catalyst, operating to improve the contact between them and the layman – to open up the closed mind.

The Society is not an adult education group, not a tract distributor, not an evangelical body, not a psychiatric movement, not propagandist. It will sometimes suggest conclusions, but doesn't mind in the least if different conclusions are reached, so long as people get the thinking habit. If it must be labelled, it is perhaps best described as a non-profit publisher and no-fee collector, co-ordinator and distributor of data. This is a modest activity, aimed only at preparing the ground. It is not by itself likely to effect great reforms. But it will change today's position, in which the general absence of accurate information and general lack of careful thought combine to *block* reform; and sometimes to lead us into deep water.

Here is a Re-Appraisal Society discussion sheet. It is a typical oversimplification, an attempt to summarize this book in a few sentences. The reader may care to observe his reactions to it. He will find that he reads quite different things into it after he has read the book. As a discussion sheet, for which it was prepared, it is useful. As a substitute for reading the book, it has little value.

L11. Essential Facts on Road Accidents

(1) Most road accidents involving deaths are caused by wild drivers, people who have temporarily lost all sense of danger and self-restraint. Prominent among these, to differing degree in different countries, are drunks and wild youths. This applies whether the dead are drivers, passengers, or pedestrians.

(2) The only established method of holding these wild drivers in check is by police intimidation. Propaganda can reach everyone if sufficient money is spent but is almost completely ineffective when these bad moods descend.

(3) The most effective form of police intimidation is by increased patrols. Unfortunately the cost is extremely high – on Smeed's figures (Ref. B3) for England, about £7,000 per life saved; probably higher in U.S.A., perhaps $30,000; less in Australia, perhaps $10,000.

(4) A cheaper form of police intimidation is the creation of a sense of police ' omnipresence '. Effective methods are available for this. Sensational results, even to the complete elimination of deaths for several months, have occasionally been achieved. Mostly politicians fear such methods however, as savouring of the ' police state '.

(5) Complete success in the elimination of habitual wild drivers would have no great effect on the total number of road accidents – probably less than 5 % reduction.

(6) Ordinary accidents, involving injury, are around 25 times as common as accidents involving death, and their toll in terms of human misery and in terms of finance is enormously greater.

(7) The chief cause of this great bulk of road accidents is the occasional error of the ordinary driver. He becomes momentarily ' near-wild ', mostly when tired, angry or in a hurry. He does not however, completely lose his awareness of danger, and his accidents rarely involve death. One researcher says that the ordinary accident and the fatal accident have about as much in common as the common cold and cancer. Another authority, perhaps in a unique position to assess the whole scene, (Ref. B406) says ' It also appears that it is not the few with deviant behaviour which account for the major proportion of the problem, but the extremely many who behave in ways that are condoned '.

(8) Several researchers (e.g. Ref. B401) have concluded that the errors of the ordinary driver derive from over-assessment of driving skill, derived from the absence of any scoring method. No golfer can tell himself that he is plus 4 when his best round is 90. But even a really bad motorist can go 30 years without an accident, thus proving to himself how good he is. In reality he may owe his immunity chiefly to the self restraint of others.

(9) One specific solution to this is to spread the conception of ' vulnerabilities '. Once a driver has started to score his driving by counting his vulnerabilities the concept remains with him and constitutes an automatic alarm in his mind, telling him when he is becoming careless.

(10) The odds of one crash during a driver's lifetime are worse than 1 in 4. Counting vulnerabilities makes it possible for any driver to reduce these odds to 1 in 40.

If everyone reduced their vulnerabilities by only 50 % – which is extremely easy – there would be a 75 % reduction in accidents. A relatively cheap propaganda drive could achieve a substantial part of this.

(11) The wild drivers referred to in paragraph 1 rarely collide with another wild driver – nearly always with a relatively innocent but careless ordinary person. A 50 % reduction in vulnerabilities by ordinary drivers would effect a substantial reduction in fatalities. This method is both cheaper and less politically dangerous than police intimidation.

(12) It can be argued that much current propaganda does harm because it tells the man who is the real cause – the ordinary driver – that it is not him at all but a specially selected wicked group. There is no such group of any size, because *habitual* drunks and wild men are speedily eliminated either by the police or by accident.

(13) Anyone can check the foregoing by counting dangerous and well-behaved drivers, and observing vulnerabilities.

The Role of this Book

This book plays a part in these long-dated plans, by providing fuel for discussions. It is a fairly complete textbook for the ordinary man.

Many will find the subject initially complex and obscure. It is not inherently so. But the realities are far removed from current assumptions. One may legitimately ask a reader to accept a dozen new ideas straight off; but scarcely to dump a dozen old ones at a sitting.

The book has been written therefore primarily for browsing. It can be picked up at any point that catches the reader's interest. Each section is either self-contained or made complete by cross references.

The straight-through reader may be a little worried by the occasional repetitions that this method involves. I hope he will tolerate them. I hope also that he will not be too distracted by the many cross references. They can safely be ignored on the first reading.

Prefatory Remarks and Acknowledgements

The reader may ask by what authority does the author write on this subject. Who is he, and what is his standing in this field? I have endeavoured to answer this partly by an account in Chapter 3 of what led up to the book. My main recommendation, however, is that I have sat at the feet of so many experts all round the world. With great generosity they gave me the results of all their experience. The responsibility for the ultimate views is of course my own; but I have been at great pains to get them checked where possible by the many kind donors, and by many others competent to judge.

My thanks are particularly due to the following:

Chief of Police Daniel S. C. Liu, Capt. Clarence M. C. Liu, Capt. Eugene Fletcher and Sgt. John Watson of the Honolulu Police; Deputy Chief Thad E. Brown, Inspector Norman L. Rector and Inspector J. L. Fulton of the Los Angeles Police; Police Commissioner Michael J. Murphy, Assistant Chief Inspector John J. King, Capt. Salvatore Matteis, Lieut. James P. Donnelly, Sgt. Frank O'Byrne, Patrolmen Victor Frandino and John Egan of the New York Police; M. Jean Confida and M. Maurice Cagnard of the Paris Police: Mr. M. R. Pike and Mr. J. C. Cutts of the Metropolitan Police, London; Mr. W. K. Brasher, London; Mr. N. E. Beddard, R.A.C., London; Rev. H. C. Blackburne, Norfolk; Miss Elizabeth Foster, London; Mr. C. A. Franklin of the A.A., London; Mr. F. Garwood & Dr. R. J. Smeed of the Road Research Lab.; Mr. Paul Haille and Commander R. S. Hawker of ROSPA; Mr. A. M. Inglis, London; Mr. Bertram Jones of the *Daily Express*, London; Mr. R. A. Kinnersley, London; Mr. Mansfield, British Insurance Association, Mr. V. H. Carter, Royal Exchange Assurance, and Mr. T. D. Wilson, Royal Insurance Co.,; Mr. G. F. O'dell and Mr. A. E. O'dell, London; Mr. Peter Petit, London; Mr. E. J. Skillman and Mr. L. A. D. Skillman, London; Mr. Jervis Smith and Mr. W. G. Askew of the I.E.E.; Mr. J. M. McSwiney, London; Mr. Stuart Thomson London; Mr. Garth Waite of the United Kingdom Alliance; Mr. E. P. G. Wright and Mr. Hunt, Standard Telecommunications Laboratories; Mr. John Yeomans, London; Mr. T. N. Boate, American Museum of Safety; Mr. Joseph Kusaila, New York State Traffic Safety Council; Dr. James L. Malfetti and Dr. James R. Adams of the Safety Project, Teachers College, Columbia University; Dr. Leon G. Goldstein, Washington; Mr. Sydney Rosen, Los Angeles, and a number of his friends who co-operated in the tests; Capt. Geoffrey Branson, Sydney; Mr. A. G. Brehaut, Sydney; Professor T. R. Brennan, Sydney University; Mrs. S. Bunning, Sydney; Mr. R. M. Creighton, Sydney; Mr. A. M. Glen,

Sydney; The Hon. Mr. Justice M. F. Hardie, Sydney; Mr. W. W. Harrison, N.S.W. Road Safety Council; The Rt. Rev. F. O. Hulme-Moir, Sydney; Rev. B. G. Judd, Sydney; Mr. C. F. Morath, Sydney; Mr. S. C. Nielsen, Sydney; Miss Miranda Skillman, Sydney; Mr. M. W. Skillman for the French translation of the booklet, Mr. Alex Strachoff for the Dutch version, and Mrs. Charlotte Robertson for the German version.

Thanks are due also to many of the authors quoted in the bibliography, who sent me much valuable information; to the many kind friends who bore my gropings and quizzes so patiently; to the many guests whose evenings I ruined; to the many strangers, cab-drivers, bus-drivers, policemen, and so on, who gave me their ideas so helpfully; to all those who carried out the tests on vulnerability; and especially to Mr. D. H. Piper and other personal friends in London and America who, on many occasions, found time to discuss the problems with me and help me sort out my mind.

I am uniquely indebted to Dr. Malfetti whose generosity of mind gave me the initial impetus.

T. S. SKILLMAN

CHAPTER 1

Introductory

An old friend of mine set out recently from New York to commence his retirement by a long anticipated trip to Europe. It was such a happy departure. The second night out he said to his wife, 'Good-night darling,' turned over and died. The poignancy of this was devastating – the sudden transition from happy anticipation, in the full flush of living, to the dread-filled telegrams, the grievous re-arrangements and painful adjustments that eddied out to so many relatives and friends.

Yet on Christmas Day of the same year, some hundreds of people all over the world set out in just such a joyous, vital, holiday mood and met their deaths just as suddenly on the roads. From each such death there spread out just the same eddies of shock, distress and grief. Yet it doesn't seem to matter! There are so many that no one can visualize it. It is almost as if people expect the distress and grief to be less poignant to the individuals concerned, because it is happening to so many others. The police, the courts, the public, are numb with it. Two such deaths, completely wanton murder by any normal standards, were punished recently by a fine of £25.

Appeals to the public get the reaction – it won't happen to me! This is rightly so. It won't. Only once in 1,400 years driving on the average in England, 1,900 in the U.S.A., 1,100 in Australia.

This is the paradox. The thing is so real, so imperative, so close, so dreadful, if it comes. Yet it is so unlikely, so remote, that to forget about it is the only healthy reaction. To become preoccupied with it may even invite it.

Let us see if we can put this strange situation into perspective. First as to the magnitude, in terms of money. It is estimated that traffic accidents cost England £200,000,000 per annum, U.S.A. $8,000,000,000, Australia £70,000,000. If we capitalize this on a ten-year purchase basis it would mean that we would be justified in spending £1,000,000,000 in England to reduce the accidents to half or $40,000,000,000 in U.S.A. or £350,000,000 in Australia.

Next let us try to visualize the magnitude in terms of human suffering. This is harder to express. Try this.* Let us in our imagination hire a small hall in our suburb. Let us gather together our acquaintances from the neighbourhood, from all levels of society and all ages – a few old people, a few babies, and so on, until we have the hall crammed full with 200 people. Then in imagination let us get a large sledge-hammer and walk through the hall hitting everyone in turn a good heavy blow somewhere or other – in the face, on the knees, in the stomach, and so on. Some people get three of four blows. We kill about 20. When we have finished let us go up on to the dais and have a look at the spectacle. Poor old George! and Fred! and Auntie Alice – all people we *know*. Listen to the screams and watch the agonizing writhings and thrashings around. Good heavens! Look at the *blood*!

This represents the crop from the roads of New South Wales in one week, from the roads of England in one day, and from the United States every four hours.

So much for magnitude. Next as to probability. This stupendous mass of suffering and waste is still relatively speaking small – minute even! Let us take a walk down to the nearest main thoroughfare at 8.30 a.m. and watch the motorists driving to work. How superbly they handle their cars! One after another they stream along in their thousands; each one at just the right speed, just the right distance, just the right angles; each one exhibiting such skill, judgement and adroitness, and a degree of easy awareness of a hundred factors that would have had their grandparents in gibbering fits. In some communities you can watch for half an hour often and not see one example of bad driving. It takes a police patrol in London two hours to catch a single violation of the law. A million cars drive around Hyde Park Corner for one collision!

Yet it is not so many years ago – well into the first decade

* This analogy appeared in the *Sydney Mirror*. Kind permission to use it is hereby acknowledged.

of this century – that I was driving along Watling Street from St. Albans to Redbourn with my father in a horse-drawn trap when we saw coming towards us a motor-car. It approached nearer and nearer at colossal speed – probably something like 20 m.p.h. My father girded up his courage and his strength, grasped the reins firmly, and proceeded to cope with the task of passing this terrifying vehicle. Surely they could achieve a safe passage. But it was not to be. They had the whole of England's main road for space, but they hit with a crash. A wheel came off the car, the horse bolted. Everyone, including Black Bess the horse, was a nervous wreck. When the village heard about it the ladies were prostrate for days.

Later in the same village Mr. Hicks the grocer was knocked down on a corner by a passing car and suffered concussion. The whole village was shattered. Mr. Dunn the hatter, who lived nearby, presented a special mirror to be set up on the corner so that this could never happen again. Mr. Hicks dined out on it for a year after.

What a far cry from this to the England of 1935 with $2\frac{1}{2}$ million vehicles. By then a motorist could expect on the average only one collision in twelve years.

Today it is one collision in 30 years. This compared with 1935 is not an improvement of two and a half to one in driving ability but of ten to one; because the number of vehicles has quadrupled in this period. If you quadruple the number of vehicles and change nothing else the chances of any one vehicle hitting another are quadrupled. Yet in this case they have been cut to less than half! (For data see Bib. 11.) What an achievement! What a magnificent display of skill! What a record of growth and development by the motorists, the pedestrians, the children and their teachers, the police, the safety organizations, the road engineers, the car manufacturers and all the rest.

This juxtaposition of extremely high achievement, extreme improbability of disaster, and yet extreme calamity when the disaster happens, is a combination which puts quite a strain on our philosophy. We are often asked in our ordinary daily life to gamble, but the penalties involved are so much less. We gamble every time we play a game, or use a tool, or take a bath, or cook a meal; but we can face the risk of a sprained ankle, a cut finger, a slip and a bruise or a burnt hand. Road accidents are quite different. Do you swim with a shark even though he only picks one bather in 10 million to slice in half? You may walk happily on a plank across a stream. But do you when it stands over a vat of boiling oil? Just knowing that there is boiling oil beneath you makes you more likely to fall in.

This is the strange situation that makes it so difficult to achieve a wise approach to the problem of road safety. It explains, I think, why such very violent, and often violently erroneous, opinions are held. There just is not enough lay experience in the kind of thinking which this problem demands.

The reader may care to try himself out on this. When he read of one accident in 30 years he probably agreed with the phrase 'extreme improbability of disaster', especially as only about one accident in four involves serious injury. What, now, does he picture the odds for the average motorist of serious injury once in a lifetime, derived from the above figures? One in fifty? One in a hundred? No, indeed! Serious injuries will average on the above figures one in 120 driver-years. If the average man drives for 30 years of his life this makes it one in four!

This book tells how these odds can be reduced to 1 in 40 by anyone prepared to do a little thinking about his driving.

PART I

Vulnerabilities

CHAPTER 2

Probabilities of Collision

THE only kind of improvement we can hope to make in the road accident situation is to reduce probabilities. We can aim to make it less likely that a motorist will have an accident; or less likely that he will be badly hurt when he does. But short of closing the roads we cannot eliminate the risk completely, any more than we can in any other walk of life. The problem therefore boils down to an assessment of risk. We can judge any suggestion only by asking what it will do to the odds.

Let us begin therefore by taking a look at the probability structure of a collision. Collisions, either vehicle/vehicle, or vehicle/pedestrian, constitute most of the accidents (about 90% in most countries), though one-man accidents are rising everywhere (App. 2).

If we can determine by calculation, observation or even by good guessing, what effect different factors have on the risks, we will have a means of choosing what is worth doing and what is a misguided waste of effort.

A driver is not always vulnerable to a collision. For example, he is not vulnerable when he is driving along an empty road. Every time he passes another person, whether walking or driving, he becomes vulnerable, because the possibility exists that this person will make an error and produce the risk of a collision. Every time he passes a turning the possibility exists that someone unforeseen will emerge and again produce the risk of a collision. When one of these things actually happens the driver is confronted with the job of avoiding the collision. He may dodge it by putting on his brakes, sounding his horn, accelerating away from it, or just by good steering. Whether he does this successfully depends on many factors – the state of the road, his own skill, his machine, the other man's skill, and so on.

By the mere act of driving every driver has, consciously or unconsciously, formed an opinion about these risks. All the time he drives he is, consciously or unconsciously, deciding that the risks he is taking are acceptable to at least one part of his mind. Another part of his mind may well be warning him that they are too great, but the decision goes against this warning. Quite clearly therefore one limit to our success in reducing the number of his accidents is set by this judgement of his. We may work on better roads or better brakes or what you will. But this all goes for nothing if he then decides to step up his driving – higher speed, finer cornering, more overtaking, and so on – being guided by the risks as he sees them.

How does he see them? Always imperfectly! If, as he drives along, he cannot discern a particular danger in the picture before him, no decision is involved, and the risk, however great, to him is nil.

To estimate the likelihood of a collision occurring to a particular driver therefore, we need to know these things about him:

(i) How much of the danger he discerns. This quality is sometimes termed his 'visual perception' or, erroneously, 'visual acuity'. This is not a quality of eyesight but of the combination of eye and mind, so that 'perception' seems to be the more suitable word (acuity can be kept for the eyesight qualities alone). Another term for this quality appears to be 'hazards alertness' (Bib. 221).

(ii) How big a risk he judges acceptable. In other words how frequently he becomes vulnerable to a collision. I have been unable to find a generally accepted name for this quality, and have called it 'vulnerability rate'.

(iii) His skill in extricating himself when confronted by an imminent collision. In the absence of a generally accepted word for this I call it 'dodging ability'.

2.1 Visual Perception

It has been found possible to make some kind of a measurement of a driver's ability in this respect. He is shown pictures and afterwards interrogated on what he saw (Bib. 401). As can be expected, those who fail to observe, or to draw the right deductions from what they observe, do indeed in real life have more collisions on the road.

It seems to have been established (Bib. 401) that this ability may be learned unconsciously merely from experience in driving. There is reason to believe that a person who approaches driving in a positive mood, with no sense of anxiety, and with a joy in it, may absorb this knowledge and develop this ability very much quicker than those who have been brought to it in an anxious mood. We shall revert to this in studying the question of education on driving problems – which may well, unskilfully applied, do almost as much harm as good (9.10).

In this, as in most other fields of high skill, the achievement goes far beyond the powers of analysis (App. 10). For example, you sometimes hear a good driver exclaim with surprise: 'You know, I had a hunch that fellow was going to pull out without warning.' He cannot analyse how he got the hunch and he cannot tell you what produced it. But it was probably something he saw, and which he knew in his subconscious how to interpret. This uncanny ability to perceive so much in the picture comes to a driver only with time. He cannot impart more than odd glimmers of it to others. It is noticeably absent in the inexperienced and probably in the inebriated. It may possibly deteriorate in the old.

2.2 Vulnerability

There is the most surprising agreement amongst experienced drivers as to what is safe and what is an unjustifiable risk. It would seem that there is a manner of driving under any given set of circumstances which in the judgement of nearly everyone is safe *within reason*. This standard does not imply the complete elimination of risk. Probably what we are unconsciously deciding is that this is the same sort of risk as we have to accept from life in general.

I have frequently tried an experiment to check this. It is one which the reader himself can readily repeat. I call it measuring a driver's vulnerability rate. When I am being driven I ask a fellow passenger to observe what he thinks is unsafe in the chauffeur's driving and to count the number of times we become momentarily vulnerable to a collision. It is only necessary to explain 'vulnerable' as being any situation in which a collision could occur if some other party made a mistake at that moment. The result rarely throws up any disagreement whatsoever when the two observers are both experienced drivers (though there is often striking and illuminating disagreement when one or both are inexperienced).

If the existence of this common standard is really true – and I have convinced myself and many others that it is – then it is a very useful discovery. It means that we can measure the risks taken by a driver.

The vulnerability rates I have measured in this simple way vary from nil to several hundred a day. The average is about ten a day for the less experienced drivers, dropping to one or two a week for the more expert. These vulnerabilities are not evenly distributed, but come in clusters. A good driver will go for a long time without incurring any vulnerabilities, and then hit a spell of inattention or carelessness or tiredness and run up a score of four or five (and sometimes many more) in a very short time.

What represents a vulnerability to the driver we are studying constitutes a threat to any other person around at the time. If this other person makes a vulnerability at the same time and place then there may arise this sudden imminence of a collision. This I term a 'confrontation'.

By taking a few rough assumptions, it is possible to calculate from the vulnerability rate the likelihood of a confrontation. This has been done in terms of schoolboy mathematics in Appendix 3. The answer for ten vulnerabilities a day works out at about one confrontation per annum. This rough calculation is quite good enough for our purposes. It doesn't make any difference worth mentioning if it turns out to be two per annum because we are only interested in variations, not in its absolute value. We only need enough guidance to get the order of magnitude.

The qualities of personality that tend to reduce the risks accepted while driving, i.e. to keep down the vulnerability rate, are probably caution, self abnegation, courtesy, awareness of social obligations, and so on. On the other hand perhaps pugnacity, forcefulness, acquisitiveness, egocentricity, self importance, etc., could be expected to increase acceptable risks. Possibly equally significant is the mood of the moment – anger, anxiety, hysteria, slackness, tiredness, sense of urgency, and so on. One could discuss at length, as has frequently been done, the influence of such factors. It is doubtful whether a conclusion of any practical value will emerge. But what is indisputable and vastly important, is that a driver's vulnerability rate will be determined by the qualities, whatever they may be, possessed by this one driver. He and he alone will determine the probabilities.

2.3 The Confrontation

When suddenly a collision becomes imminent, and the driver must dodge away from another person, qualities quite different from the foregoing are called upon. These are presumably such things as response time, quickness in taking decision, clarity of eyesight, peripheral vision, judgement of distance and speed, muscular strength, athletic skill, muscular co-ordination, and so on. The probabilities now involved are clearly a function of these characteristics as they are possessed by both parties to the threatened collision.

The happening which calls out this transition from one set of probabilities to the other is what I have termed the 'confrontation'.

2.4 Escaping from the Confrontation

A good 'dodger' will clearly extricate himself from more confrontations than will a bad one. But the result will still be very dependent on the other man. Under certain conditions of loss of control, some drivers and some pedestrians are undodgeable. Great skill and ability by one driver therefore will not diminish the odds by as big a factor as it does in the situation prior to confrontation. In other words the probabilities of an outstandingly good man meeting another outstandingly good man to help him out are small, and the odds of a collision are dominated by the performance of the average man.

If we select just one of the skills that contribute towards dodging, such as the quality of good eyesight or quick reaction, then this one characteristic will play even less part in changing the probabilities. It would be good fun to draft out a learned mathematical analysis of all this, but it would be quite unnecessary. The basic reasoning is quite inescapable and is, moreover, confirmed by any number of investigations (e.g. Bib. 401, Bib. 1 Chapter 4).

My own guess is that the average driver fails to escape about 5% of his confrontations and that the spread of this figure is not very great – say from about 2% to 10%. If the average motorist meets, as is estimated above, one confrontation a year, and escapes 19 confrontations out of 20, then the average motorist will have a collision once in 20 years which lines up fairly well with the reality.

Please do not be shocked at the thought of a guess in this matter. None of our conclusions will be affected if I am several hundred per cent wrong. In any case a most thorough and expensive analysis would be no more trustworthy. There are too many unknown factors and too many variables. This is one of the great handicaps in tackling the whole problem of road accidents. Very few conclusions are capable of clear proof.

You may care to check my guess from your own experience. How often is the squeal of brakes that heralds a confrontation followed by the crash that announces a collision? If you say one in ten or one in five instead of my one in twenty, it will not affect the conclusions towards which I am leading you.

2.5 'Susceptibility' of the Odds

The broad principle governing the probabilities should now be clear. The vital question is how 'susceptible' are the odds. Clearly some factors can influence them profoundly whereas others will have very little impact. Let us take a few cases to illuminate this.

Consider two imaginary drivers who are identical in all respects save visual perception. If driver A has poor visual perception and fails to see half the dangers, while driver B sees them all, then A will tot up twice as many vulnerabilities and his odds of a confrontation will be twice B's.

Similarly, if driver A *for any other reason* tots up twice as many vulnerabilities as B, his odds of a confrontation will be twice B's.

If driver A becomes drunk or emotionally upset, he may compensate for this by being extra careful and clock up no more vulnerabilities than when he is normal. Or he may become irresponsible and be vulnerable ten times as frequently as B, in which case his odds of a confrontation are again ten times as great as B's.

So far we have been talking about confrontations, not collisions. If A and B have the same risks of a confrontation, no matter for what different reasons, it is unlikely as already pointed out, that the odds of a collision will vary very much between them. This is because the odds in the second stage of the collision are so much less susceptible to influence by any particular characteristic. They are dependent on driver or pedestrian C – the other party to the collision – as well as A or B. Only a truly drastic reduction in the dodging ability of one party – such as one or the other being seriously drunk – could make a significant change in the odds. This is why the accuracy of the estimates given in the previous section is unimportant.

2.6 Deductions

The key to reducing collisions therefore lies clearly in reduction of vulnerability rate, either by improving the driver's visual perception; or by improving his judgement of risk. It is in this area that the odds are most 'susceptible' and we can be sure of getting results from what we do.

If a driver sees by direct observations of himself that he is taking about 3,600 risks per annum, and that cutting this down to 1,800 will halve his chances of an accident (and also halve his chances of getting killed) he will not need a lot of persuading to make the cut. From the salesman's or psychologist's point of view it is much easier to reach his mind on this than by talking about being more careful, more unselfish, better mannered, etc.

If everyone made a 50% reduction in vulnerabilities, then the collisions on the roads would drop not by 50% but by 75%. This is because not only is any one driver vulnerable half as often, but the number of threats he meets from all other drivers is also reduced to half. Therefore the odds of a confrontation are reduced to a quarter. The odds of a collision arising from a confrontation can be anything – one in five or one in fifty without in any way affecting the above. If you cut the confrontations to a quarter, the collisions must be reduced in the same proportion.

CHAPTER 3

Story of an Investigation

3.1 Tentative Beginnings

WHEN I first stumbled on this conception of vulnerability I went around asking all sorts of people how many times a day on the average did the average motorist become vulnerable to an accident. The degree of agreement in the replies was astonishing. No one said less than one per day; hardly anyone above 20; the general feeling was about 10. Very few made much difficulty about the idea, or produced difficulties about the definition of vulnerability. Very quickly it became clear that a common standard existed, as described in Chapter 2. It looked as if I had a new weapon in the struggle to understand what was happening on the roads.

I then started trying to measure the vulnerability rates of everyone with whom I drove. To my surprise I found this quite easy. Whenever I went driving with someone else I put a few odd visiting cards in my breast pocket. Every time I judged they had become vulnerable I moved a card from my breast pocket to my side pocket. If a big score was made in a short time, I wrote the number on a card. At the end of the journey I counted the cards.

There was rarely much doubt as to whether a vulnerability occurred if it was a momentary one. I had some difficulty in rating a continuing vulnerability, such as over-fast driving or driving too near the kerb, but finally adopted the idea of counting one vulnerability for each car or pedestrian who came within range of an accident while the dangerous speed persisted. This seemed to give excessive scores, but at least lined up fairly well with the widely held conviction that speed is indeed one of the greatest dangers.

The results of these tentative measurements were astonishingly enlightening, in spite of their obvious inaccuracies. One driver with whom I felt specially safe averaged less than one vulnerability per week. Some drivers who had always seemed dangerous to me clocked over 50 and sometimes hundreds of vulnerabilities on every journey I made with them. The average was indeed about 10. (This was in Australia. Later in England and the U.S.A. it seems nearer 5.) The figure of 10 vulnerabilities per day and one collision in 20 years meant that the average number of vulnerabilities which a driver experienced before he had a crash was about 70,000. This meant that I had stumbled on something which happens about 70,000 times as frequently as an accident and which is clearly related to the number of accidents. Moreover, it is measurable for any particular individual. It seemed that such a concept could solve many of the difficulties experienced in research. For example, if we attempt to relate a driver's personal characteristics not to the number of accidents he has but to something that happens 70,000 times as frequently, it is going to be very much easier to collect statistics which will have some 'significance' (App. 5), and draw conclusions which are worth backing. One person looking at vulnerability rates can collect as much data in a month as 20 people could in a year working on accidents.

So I started observing the vulnerabilities of different kinds of driver, and of drivers in different states of mind. The results were, to me, sensational. For example, I think I found (one can't be very sure) one driver whose vulnerability rate went up to crazy figures when he was angry; and another whose vulnerability was reduced by anger. Ideas that were completely new to me began to emerge. For instance I found a certain kind of embitterment – what the Australian describes as 'bloody-mindedness' – went with a high vulnerability rate. Perhaps this is what is sometimes called the extra-punitive characteristic. (Bib. 401 p. 8.) Perhaps the most striking results were the incredibly high figures produced by youths (not nearly so much by young women). One young man had a crash while I was observing him and his vulnerability rate then dropped from hundreds a day to nil and appeared to stay there. The reason in his case was just money – the high cost of his crash, with no insurance cover.

3.2 Three Surprising Propositions

Certain conclusions become very hard to avoid:

(a) *Some Drivers are Unaware of any Danger*

It appeared that certain drivers on occasion made themselves vulnerable hundreds of times in one trip. Such total unawareness of danger is hard to believe. It certainly is not very common, and it seems rarely to be habitual; but it does happen.

This is confirmed by the existence of accident-prone motorists – or so-called 'accident-repeaters'. Many of these are the product of a run of bad luck, or disappear from the scene for other reasons (see 10.4). But some do persist, so there is no doubt that some people really do drive in such a way that they deservedly average several accidents a year. As the general rate is only about one accident in 30 years, these people must operate at about 100 times the normal vulnerability rate.

Such stupefying unawareness must result also in their taking risks of a different kind from the errors of the ordinary motorist. If they can't see ordinary dangers they are likely on occasion to lay themselves open to graver dangers than the ordinary man would ever run into. They could be expected to contribute much more than the average therefore to the really violent accidents.

This also is confirmed by the accident data. For example, drunks, who appear to be the largest proportion of the high vulnerability group, figure in most districts in only 1 or 2% of ordinary accidents but in 30 to 40% of fatalities (12.13). Research confirms that the whole structure of fatal accidents appears fundamentally different from that of ordinary ones (Bib. 306).

The mental abnormalities which must be associated with this fantastic unawareness make it nearly certain that these people will not be amenable to any appeal. We can be sure that the improvement we can get by trying to work on their minds will be disappointing.

This problem is considered further in 10.4.

(b) *The Ordinary Driver is the Culprit*

The second conclusion which emerged is that the motorist who drives wildly is very rare. A great many borderline vulnerabilities can be observed, but very few violent ones. If we take the violent vulnerability as indicative of the wild driver then it is only necessary to take a number of cross sections of the traffic to get an indication of his prevalence. We may do this by standing on an awkward corner that tends to show up bad driving. We can also check it while out driving ourselves by asking a passenger to count the total number of cars that pass while another passenger or the driver looks out for any error that could be classed as violent. Such observations seem to indicate that in England about one driver in a thousand could be classified as wild; and in N.S.W. one in five hundred. (Insufficient data for U.S.A.)* There does not appear to be a noticeable difference between observations on main country roads and observations in the city.

Wild drivers disappear almost completely when a policeman is conspicuous on a corner or when a recognizable police car is on the road. Police still do catch the wild driver of course, but only when he hasn't seen them. The rareness of wild drivers can also be established from police data (App. 13).

It is much more difficult to determine what proportion of these wild drivers are habituals. One would expect that the habitually wild drivers would be eliminated either by police or by accidents and there is much evidence to support this. Certainly a considerable proportion of the wild drivers are ordinary motorists making a rare error.

In making such observations it is important to ignore cases which are inconsiderate but not dangerous. Discourtesy, which makes us all angry, is not to be confused with dangerous driving, even though it may lead the less mature victims to drive more dangerously themselves.

These observations lead us to the most surprising deduction: a thousand ordinary motorists averaging 5 to 10 vulnerabilities per day will produce a far greater total number of dangers than one habitually dangerous driver, even if the dangerous driver

---

* Later observations in New York and Los Angeles indicate that for most of the week the figure is well above 1 in 2000.

clocks up several hundred vulnerabilities a day. In other words, the authorities have been so successful in toning down or eliminating the dangerous ones that the ordinary man, because of his prevalence, emerges today as the chief cause of accidents.

(c) *Work on the Ordinary Driver Gives the Best Yield*

If there are a thousand ordinary drivers to one habitually wild one who makes 100 times the vulnerabilities, the collisions will be apportioned on the following basis (assuming completely random juxtapositions):

Normal /Normal	100 ordinary accidents.
Normal /Wild	10 violent accidents.
Wild /Wild	1 violent accident.

If we could work on the habitually wild drivers (a nearly impossible assignment) and reduce their vulnerabilities to half, we will reduce the 10 violent accidents to 5, but we would make no impression on the 100 ordinary accidents.

If instead we work on the ordinary driver (surely not so difficult an objective) and reduce his vulnerabilities to half we would not only make the same improvement of 50% in the 10 violent accidents, but we would also reduce the 100 ordinary accidents to 25 (half the vulnerabilities meeting half the threats).

This explains why even a most intensive drive on drunks (see, for example 6.2) has no noticeable effect on the total number of accidents.

3.3 Journey Round the World

The foregoing three propositions were so astonishing, that I decided in 1964 to take the investigation further, and endeavour to make a general survey in a number of countries (a journey that kept me away from home for over eleven months). I asked an old friend, Police Chief Dan Liu of Honolulu for help. When I called on him he had on his desk a report that had arrived that very morning, covering a three-year investigation made by the Department of Health, Hawaii, and sponsored by the Department of Health, Education and Welfare, Washington, D.C., under the leadership of Dr. Robert A. Spicer. (Bib. 401). It seemed at first sight to record almost entirely negative results. But when I got down to it I was electrified to find what seemed to be specific confirmation of the ideas set out in Chapter 2. Where everyone had assumed there would be a specific relationship between certain driver characteristics (such as aggressiveness) and the number of accidents for such drivers, the study had found none – with the one exception already referred to of visual perception. (For other confirmation of this see Bib. 406.)

With the encouragement from the Spicer report and with very helpful introductions from Chief Liu, I then visited various Police Departments, Safety Authorities and Research Centres of the United States, England and Europe. I found a surprising readiness to give my ideas a hearing. I have acknowledged part of my debt in the Preface, but I doubt if I can convey what a sensational and dramatic experience this was. I wonder if many people have any conception of the size of the world effort that is being made on this problem. There are safety groups in all the police forces, road safety officers in local authorities, national and regional safety councils, university groups, motorists' associations, insurance interests, oil interests, manufacturers' interests – all devoting money and staff to it. Several large laboratories exist. So many new conceptions and different slants of view poured in from these that my own picture grew more and more confused and uncertain. One is overwhelmed with the data and by one's inability to distil anything out of it.*

Wherever I went I talked to people about it. Every taxi driver, every visitor to my home, anyone I met in a train – they were all quizzed. I never met anyone who wasn't interested, and no one without strong opinions. There was never the slightest difficulty in getting people to talk.

3.4   The Prime Cause of Accidents

As I continued to work, one factor emerged more and more clearly. This is the unconscious arrogance of nearly all drivers. I hardly ever met a driver without a pet theory, or one who didn't know precisely why accidents happened and what should

---

* Perhaps the only adverse comment is the lack of world co-ordination. Many of the groups are quite unaware of the work being done by others.

be done. Rarely indeed, was the pet theory valid. I only once in the whole world met a male driver who thought his driving ability was below average (50% must be, of course) and even there it was only a line of talk. He didn't really believe it. The picture could not be conveyed better than in Dr. Spicer's own words, which rang a bell when I first read them and have since taken over nearly the whole belfry.

'... A factor that turned up repeatedly is one which in a sense could be the key to understanding the horrible highway slaughter. This human factor is the almost self evident but rarely noted condition; viz., due to the absence of reliable criteria or standards, the typical driver has no dependable method for assessing his own driving ability! This condition is exacerbated further by his own exaggerated emotional involvement in driving and his belief in the myth that 'anyone' can drive a car. So he operates his vehicle day after day blissfully ignorant of the tragic disparity that might exist between his idealized self concept and reality. This illusion is further compounded by the state-licensing which makes him legally a 'good' driver, and by the many other misleading data such as few traffic tickets, small number of accidents (it's the other man's fault anyway), and his own peerless self appraisal. Incredibly high self estimates of drivers were found throughout. This absurd self-concept is reinforced daily as the driver 'successfully' gets from one point to another day after day. The absence of proper training, examinations, probation periods, periodic checks, and *clearly defined driver criteria* in a sense make the driver his own worst enemy. A bowler, a golfer, a rifle man all have dependable scoring methods that truthfully define their competence – not so the hapless driver.'

Another factor which obtruded itself was the psychological comfort and sense of refuge or compensation which many people derive from their cars. A man having to eat dirt from employer or employees, or from wife or children, recovers his self respect in his car. It is often his only escape, the one place where things go right, the one spot where he can lick his wounds and regain his serenity; or the one avenue where he can feel big without someone trying to cut him down to size. It is his personal possession, often more completely than any other thing in his life. Similarly, the youth who cuts no ice with the girls, the man who sees no financial success ahead, the Walter Mittys and the Mr. Pollys rebelling from a humdrum life, – for all these the car is often their only really satisfying daily experience. It becomes disproportionately important to many a man. Nothing must be allowed to intrude into his dream. The suggestion that he might not be a perfect driver threatens it, and is immensely painful.

If all this is true – and there seems very little doubt that it is – then the first move in any attempt to reduce traffic accidents is to find a way of reaching these closed minds. There are of course many ways being tried – education, persuasion, intimidation, propaganda directed towards fear of a crash, propaganda towards self-abnegation and social duty, and so on.

A motorist who is normally reasonable may also close his mind and get the bit between his teeth, due to a fit of anger or frustration or when agitated or in a hurry. While in this state he is likely to be just as much a source of danger as any foolish poseur.

What I began to wonder, especially in view of Dr. Spicer's paragraph above, was whether there might not be another method of reaching the closed minds, using the idea of measuring vulnerability rate. After all, everyone is interested in his own score at almost anything. All the newspaper and magazine quizzes show this. 'How good a Husband are you?', or Boss, or Employee, etc. This apparently does not offend the ego, because everyone enters into it in the hope – and generally in the expectation – that they will make a flattering score. The idea was supported by frequent diagnoses of 'inattention' as a major contributory cause of accidents. Surely anything which caused the driver to think about driving as he drove could do nothing but good.

It seemed, too, that anything which started people thinking or talking about vulnerabilities could well be effective in reducing vulnerabilities, even if the ego were too tender for them to take a score. I was much encouraged in this by kind help and information from Dr. Malfetti of Columbia University and from M. Confida and M. Cagnard of the Paris Police Force.

3.5 The Vulnerability Experiment

So I set up a small scale experiment. This was limited to self-measurement. I had (and still have) grave doubts of anything which encouraged outside criticism – for example wives measuring husbands' vulnerabilities. One could imagine the back seat driver suddenly acquiring a very stinging multi-lashed whip by this means. Methods were suggested therefore whereby a driver could measure his vulnerabilities without anyone else being aware that he was doing it.

The great unresolved question was whether it would be economically possible to present the ideas to the average motorist in an acceptable form. If it were, a substantial reduction in accident rate might be within reach.

A booklet was prepared and distributed to a small representative selection of motorists along with a questionnaire. The booklet is reproduced below (3.6). It is worth reading because it presents the arguments of the foregoing sections in a somewhat simpler form. It was intentionally dogmatic, with a view to securing maximum immediate acceptance by the general public. This made it sometimes a little irritating to the more experienced recipient, who recognized that some of the statements were over-simplified or unproven.

Many suggestions for improvement in this booklet were received, and are incorporated in the version below. The major error was the assumption that drivers' vulnerability rates are more or less constant. The earlier experiments had all indicated that this was so, but had concentrated on less skilled drivers. The better drivers, with more experience, appear to go a long time without incurring any vulnerabilities at all, and yet still make quite a poor average by incurring a whole cluster at a time when they are overtired or in a hurry.

The object of the experiment was not so much to confirm the ideas (which were considered proven) as to test out the booklet. It is clear that better methods than the distribution of a booklet can be devised; but probably nothing so cheap.

Nothing very sensational was expected. No one move has made much impression at any stage. The 90% improvement referred to in Chapter 1 is the result of many small moves, each taken with much effort and expense. 1% is a good yield. There has never been a panacea and there is less likely to be one as we get down to the hard core. Nevertheless, the result of this small experiment, as set out in Chapter 4, indicated that a 10% improvement might well be achieved quite cheaply by a general distribution of the booklet – a relatively enormous yield! Even larger yields are possible by further measures considered later.

Here then is the booklet, which properly distributed can save many lives and much distress:

3.6 Text of Booklet on Vulnerabilities

Note: This booklet is available in French, German and Dutch.

(a) *How to Avoid a Collision*

All drivers at times make themselves momentarily vulnerable to an accident. They take a chance; or fail to observe a potential danger; or attention momentarily wanders; or the automatic pilot in the brain (which skilled drivers use for most of the time) has a minor malfunction. Even the best drivers do this from time to time, particularly when over-tired. Less skilled drivers are vulnerable as often as 50 times a day. The average is about 5 to 10 a day.

If one of these vulnerabilities happens to coincide in time and space with that of another driver then a collision will be imminent. Such a juxtaposition happens to the average driver about once a year. This means that he makes about 3–4,000 misjudgements before one catches up with him.

Once the juxtaposition of two vulnerabilities (a confrontation) has happened, it is no longer completely within the power of either driver to escape a collision. Each is dependent on the skill and co-operation of the other. Nineteen out of twenty such juxtapositions are successfully handled on the average by the two drivers. The twentieth produces a crash.

Every time another driver makes himself vulnerable he also constitutes a threat to you. It doesn't matter very much whether he is a worthy citizen making a rare error, or a drunken lunatic taking chances all the time. The pain and damage are much the same.

You can therefore picture yourself as driving through a crowd of such vulnerabilities, or threats, rather like driving through a swarm of flies. Having an accident is a matter of chance, like getting one of the flies in your eye. You are not much concerned with where that particular fly comes from. On this analogy making yourself vulnerable can be likened to sticking your head outside the windscreen, so that the flies can get in your eye.

There are three ways of escaping the fly in your eye (i.e. a collision), under these conditions: (*a*) Abolish the flies, (*b*) Dodge when you see one coming, and (*c*) Don't stick your head out.

Most schemes for improving safety have concentrated on the 'abolish the flies' technique. 'Stop drunken drivers', 'catch the violators of the law', 'punish the slow driver, or the fast driver, or the lane changer', and so on. This is sound, but drunken drivers, law violators and other wild drivers are already in a very small minority. Nearly all drivers are sober, careful and truly anxious not to violate the law or have an accident. Yet they all make these occasional lapses into vulnerability. If all the habitually wild and dangerous drivers on the road were eliminated it would make no great reduction in the number of threats facing you as you drive along, nor in the number of accidents.

Many research workers have concentrated on solution (*b*). How well can you dodge? How good is your response time? Or your peripheral vision? Do you have an impulsive temperament? Can you take quick decisions? How good are the roads? and so on. The answers to such questions, while of considerable value, will not eliminate the element of chance that faces you every time you go out driving. In dodging you are still dependent on what the other fellow does.

Why not try solution (*c*)? Don't stick your head out so often. This is entirely within your own power. If you cut the number of times you stick your head out to half, that will halve the chances of an accident for you. The way to do it is to count your vulnerabilities, and then set out to cut them in half – which you will find is extraordinarily easy to do. If you do this and no one else on the roads does anything, you will have halved your own risks, i.e. you can expect to go twice as many years without a crash. If all other careful motorists do the same, then clearly the number of crashes in the whole community will be reduced to nearly a quarter (half the number of vulnerabilities meeting half the number of threats).

Is it not an exciting and reassuring discovery that it is within the power of the careful motorists to do this, without being dependent at all on the co-operation of the wild and dangerous ones? The only accidents we cannot diminish by this means are those between two wild ones. Somehow this does not seem to matter so much – almost a kind of justice. Anyway, a good crash often turns a wild driver into a safe one.

(b) *Preliminary Run*

Putting the foregoing into practice is a matter only of observing yourself as you drive. Carry in your pocket a small clicker-counter, and operate it each time you observe that you have become momentarily vulnerable. When you empty your pocket at the end of the day you will automatically come across the clicker. Record your score and record also a quick guess on the day's mileage.

Instead of a clicker you can use a dozen pieces of card, such as visiting cards. Put them in your breast pocket each morning and transfer one to a side pocket each time you become vulnerable. They also automatically show up when you empty your pockets at night, and remind you to enter your score.

To start with you will probably find it difficult to decide when you are vulnerable. You are not likely to make any glaring errors while you are concentrating on observing yourself, so your score for the first day might well be nil. But as you continue to think about it you will see possibilities of accidents, if someone else is only foolish enough, at every corner. You will be inclined to say you are vulnerable hundreds of times a day, and perhaps want to give up the exercise.

Academically speaking, you are indeed vulnerable every instant you drive. For example a child can dart out of *any* area, or from behind *any* parked car. You clearly cannot drive on this assumption, or you would never take out your car. The test in this case is – if you did happen to kill a child, would you blame yourself? If it happened in a street where you can see a lot of children playing you probably would. If it were on a main highway where children were not to be expected, you would probably not feel guilty.

The test then must be purely in relation to your own judgement. In determining whether you made a vulnerability you may ask yourself the following two questions:

(a) If at that moment some foolish person had done the wrong thing would I have been threatened with an accident? If the answer is Yes, then:

(b) If this foolish person had come along and caused an accident at that moment, would I have blamed myself afterwards, not for the accident, but for taking the risk?

This is the kind of assessment you make more or less unconsciously in every aspect of living. The exercise of so-called 'wisdom' and 'judgement' is often largely an unconscious estimation of probability.

Clearly you must not consider whether you would be in the right; only whether it is reasonable in your judgement to take a chance that someone else, drunk or sober, good or bad, will not be there and in the wrong at that particular moment.

Do not count your violations of the law, unless the result could be a crash. (This does not mean that you are entitled to ignore the law. There are many good reasons for co-operating with the authorities besides direct avoidance of a crash.)

There are some situations, such as too high a speed, where the vulnerabilities are not momentary but persist for some time. Under these conditions clearly every pedestrian, vehicle, animal, etc., which is passed represents a separate vulnerability and should be counted. Any of these at any time could make a mistake, and if this occurs at the moment of passing at too high a speed then a confrontation ensues. To take another example, if you drive past 20 parked cars in a busy shopping centre so close that anyone opening an offside door would hit you, then you have been vulnerable 20 times – because you know quite well that at any car a busy shopper could have opened a door just as you were passing, and created a confrontation.

(c) *Scoring Your Vulnerabilities*

Take the daily score for a period of three weeks. Make no attempt to change your driving habits for the first week. The week's score gives you a base line. Make the second week a super-safe one. Set out to cut the score to an absolute minimum, accepting any delay for the sake of safety. At the end of the second week review the sacrifices you have made, and decide which of them are acceptable and which you are simply not prepared (for any reason whatever) to incorporate in your driving technique. Drive for the third week on this basis.

If your score for the third week is substantially better than your first, you can feel confident that you have substantially reduced your chances of a crash.

If you find after a few days that you incur very few vulnerabilities, it is quite in order to accept this and not go trying to find them. Most careful, experienced drivers only incur vulnerabilities when they are tired or in a hurry. Instead of taking observations for a full week, then, two days would be enough if you select days when a great deal of driving is done. The observation should be particularly careful towards the end of the journey when you are getting tired. You may also care to make especially acute observations when you are in a great hurry. The available evidence suggests that the number of vulnerabilities incurred at the end of a long day or when under great pressure can easily be ten or twenty times the normal. They seem to come in clusters – perhaps four or five in ten minutes.

You may experience a considerable resistance within your mind to making these observations when tired or hurried; but you should be encouraged to make the effort by the thought that this is likely to be of considerable protective value, not only during the experiment but as a matter of habit.

(d) *Unavoidable Risks*

Part of your regular driving may involve crossing traffic streams at points where vulnerability is inevitable. In such cases get out a map and mark out a route such that during the second (ultra-safe) week you always turn *with* the traffic stream, and never cross it, even if this adds miles to your driving. After all, this is only for a week. You may be surprised at what a comfort the extra safety is, and find yourself ready to accept it by the end of the week.

If you feel vulnerable all the time you are on a high speed road, examine whether this is because you drive too near the car ahead. If so, try keeping a safe distance away during the second (ultra-safe) week. Each time some foolish driver cuts in to the space which you have left, give him best and drop back again to a safe distance. Count the number of cut-ins. It may not be as bad as you expect. In estimating what distance is safe, allow for the other foolish driver on your tail. After all, the existence of fools is part of life, and not something to discover anew each time you go out. There is really no reason why you should allow anyone to force you to risk a crash if you don't want it.

If you feel vulnerable only because of speed, ask yourself whether this is justified. On a one-way road averaging 70 m.p.h. the speed difference between cars is probably not more than 30 m.p.h., whereas on a two-way road averaging 30 m.p.h. the speed difference is often 80 m.p.h. (40 m.p.h. each, in opposite directions). It may be almost as bad, by damaging confidence, to imagine unreal vulnerabilities as to fail to see real ones.

(e) *Limitations*

The foregoing suggestions are not a cure for all ills. They do not protect from the remote dangers or the mechanical failures. But they do give a substantial improvement in your chances as far as the most common classes of accidents are concerned – the collision between two vehicles, a car hitting a pedestrian, and a car running off the road.

Observation of vulnerabilities is not a substitute for the endeavours to curb wild and drunken drivers. These efforts supplement each other by working on different factors in the probability structure.

It should not be overlooked that without the present efforts of the authorities on many fronts a suitable probability picture could not exist, and the above procedures would be meaningless.

We said earlier that it didn't matter very much whether the driver who caused your accident was producing a large number of vulnerabilities or only a few. It's the one that hits you that matters. This needs some qualification, because the man who makes many vulnerabilities is clearly unaware of the dangers. The accidents he causes therefore tend to be more violent. As an example, drunks were involved in 33–38% of fatal accidents in New York recently, but in less than 2% of all the accidents.

Reducing the vulnerabilities of the ordinary driver will reduce in the same proportion both the ordinary accidents and the violent or fatal accidents. Working on the wild man – even if it were possible – will not have a similar overall effect.

(f) *Use of the Vulnerability Conception in Ordinary Driving*

Most of those who have carried out the three weeks test find that the awareness of vulnerabilities remains. They discover themselves discussing particular cases with their passengers or other motorists. As a result any unusual sequence of vulnerabilities on their part is immediately noticed.

Thus an automatic alarm has been planted in their minds, warning them when their driving is getting dangerous.

Those who do not have this reaction at first will get reminded of the concept when in due course they experience a near-miss or when they see an accident. It is a seed that cannot easily be eliminated from even the most disinterested mind. Sooner or later they start observing their vulnerabilities.

The habit of observing vulnerabilities, and perhaps making a check count every few months, is helped by some kind of reminder in the car. An electrical counter operated from a push button and mounted on the dashboard, or plugged in the cigarette lighter socket, seems the ideal solution.

For reasons that are elaborated in the Re-Appraisal Society's book 'How to Reduce Road Accidents'* it seems clear that awareness of vulnerabilities will remain when a motorist gets the bit between his teeth, due to hurry, anger, etc. It thus appears to be an excellent way of planting an inhibition in the mind which will operate to override the basic antisocial motivations. If a sufficient number of motorists therefore can be persuaded to think along these lines, the most sensational reduction in the hard core of accidents can be expected.

(End of Booklet)

* This book (4.8, 6.1 and 7.2).

CHAPTER 4

Results of the 'Vulnerability' Experiment

SEVENTY-SIX copies of the booklet and questionnaire were sent out, and forty-two replies were received. These were divided between England, U.S.A. and Australia. Some recipients were traffic specialists, or psychologists, some were technical men with a mathematical bent, and the majority were, as nearly as possible, typical motorists of varying skill.

Whether the results are meaningful with such a small sampling clearly depends upon the skill with which the samples are selected and weighted. The sampling problem is much simpler than, for example, an Election Opinion Poll, for two reasons. Firstly, motorists are a much more homogeneous group than electors. Their objectives are all the same. So are their feelings when frustrated. Therefore a smaller cross-section is sufficient to give a lead. Secondly, we are not looking for 49–51% accuracy, but only a general trend. An error of 20% would not affect the guidance which we get (App. 5).

4.1 Reduction in Vulnerability Rate

Twenty-two people (29%) attempted to carry out the tests. Eleven of them (14%) achieved a substantial reduction in vulnerability rate. Average reduction 40%. This would indicate that if we approached all motorists we could expect to achieve a reduction in accidents of $11\frac{1}{2}\%$. (In place of 100 vulnerabilities meeting 100 threats, we could expect to achieve 86 + 60% of 14 = 94 vulnerabilities meeting 94 threats, i.e. odds of 94 × 94 instead of 100 × 100 = $11\frac{1}{2}\%$ improvement.) This is a really valuable improvement.

The vulnerability rates reported varied between 0 and 42 per week, with an average of about 20 (i.e. 3 a day).

Checking back to the recipients later it became clear that

we had made several errors in approach, notably in failing to suggest prior discussions and in implying that the vulnerabilities are regular, whereas in reality they come in clusters, and scarcely at all while the observer is on the *qui vive* to find them. It is hoped that research organizations will repeat and develop these experiments. The above $11\frac{1}{2}\%$ could rise to at least 20% using the modified booklet plus some prior discussion.

Some evidence appeared that the less safe drivers took to these ideas much better than safe drivers. They immediately got a score, whereas the good ones found it a little unreal. The effect on the total number of accidents of reducing 20 vulnerabilities to 10 is clearly 10 times as much as reducing 2 vulnerabilities to 1. Consequently there is some reason to believe that in practice the results might be sensationally larger than the above calculations indicate.

Allowance has to be made for the fact that a good deal of chasing had to be undertaken to get these results in. Also for the fact that being asked to participate in a test arouses much more interest than receiving a booklet through the mail. There is therefore not much 'significance' in the figure of 29% for those who responded. On the other hand, the figure of 14% for those who did the tests successfully would have been considerably higher with the improved booklet.

The reduction of 40% in vulnerability rate is of much greater significance, because once those concerned had decided to do the test then they were working under much the same conditions as the general body of motorists would, i.e. in this respect they were a representative set of samples. The test firstly demonstrated quite convincingly that a reduction in his own risks of at least 40% is within the reach of any motorist who is interested. Secondly, it suggested that the best drivers achieve a vulnerability rate less than one-tenth of the average. It also demonstrated that the booklet is basically sound and does get the ideas over.

4.2 Opinions on the Scheme

Most doubts about the whole scheme came from specialists,

especially the police, almost entirely on the grounds that the public would not respond.

There was also a reaction against the scheme from the mathematically minded, who found the approximations far too rough and ready. In this I have little doubt that the mathematicians were wrong, and that they were trying to apply unsuitable techniques.

The majority of recipients, representing the general public, were almost all enthusiastically in favour of the idea. Yet surprisingly their one-year estimate of public response was even lower than that of the specialists. The question asked was: 'What percentage of drivers could be persuaded to measure their vulnerability rate and to try to reduce it, given a good propaganda campaign?' The answers averaged as follows:

	Ordinary Motorists	Specialists
Within a year	13%	18%
Within five years	29%	28%

4.3 Effect of Tiredness

Several experimenters reported increased vulnerability rates when tired. E. J. Skillman finds that the condition of the driver at the start of a journey is the most important factor. He estimates the vulnerabilities of a driver who starts a long journey fresh could, at the last part of the journey, be ten times what they are at the start, assuming there are no stops. If the driver starts tired, the comparable figures at the end could be 50 times as great. He finds that the vulnerabilities ultimately go up so fast that in effect for any particular set of conditions there is a maximum safe driving distance, beyond which it is unwise to drive at all.

I understand that some traffic observations on the Newark–New York route seem to confirm this. Much of the traffic on this route is to and from towns which are just too far away for a one-day drive, but drivers tend to push themselves to get home for the night. I understand that the accidents on the last stretch, in the one direction only, show a sharp rise at the end of the day.

This suggests a campaign along the lines of 'When your vulnerabilities rise stop for the night.'

I have been unable to locate any data co-relating accident frequency with the distance driven prior to the crash. It is not a required item on standard police reports of accidents.*

4.4 Psychological Resistance

Many drivers discovered in themselves a strong and puzzling resistance to making the tests. Others made comments which seemed to indicate that they were also experiencing some internal resistance that they did not recognize. For example, several said, though not in so many words, that thinking about their driving would distract them from their driving. Others said that moving a card from one pocket to the other was distracting, or dangerous. (Yet they probably use a handkerchief or smoke while driving and almost certainly at some time use one hand for opening a window, signalling or putting on lights or wipers.)

This mental resistance would seem to be consistent with the general overestimation of driving skill and the other emotional complications commented on in Chapter 3. There is, however, another, more probable, explanation. It was found that most experimenters with this reaction were exceptionally good drivers. Subsequent discussions revealed that in several cases they had given the scheme a trial but had failed to observe any vulnerabilities at all. They then made heavy weather of trying to find a few to oblige me. Small wonder they ultimately rejected the scheme.

The unresolved question with these drivers is, do they occasionally suffer from a cluster of vulnerabilities under exceptional conditions – when tired, or upset or preoccupied? It was clear that for them the method of measurement needs recasting. This has been covered in the revised booklet reproduced in 3.6 where it is suggested that in place of regular observation of vulnerabilities over a week, they be asked to

* There is sometimes an inquiry, driver ill or fatigued? But this is insufficient to establish the significance of the condition, especially as drivers are so frequently in a state of shock after a crash.

observe only at the end of a long day's driving. The phrase 'Measure your vulnerability rate' has been replaced by the phrase 'Count your vulnerabilities'.

4.5 Driving Skill

Estimates of own driving skill were:

Average	27%
Above Average	65%
Variable or uncertain	8%
Below average	Nil

4.6 Methods of Counting Vulnerabilities

The most favoured method of counting was a clicker built into the car, with a button on the steering-wheel. My feeling is that this would be good, provided it were out of sight of passengers. I remain very doubtful of any participation or awareness by passengers.

I have a sample of a suitable clicker, in case any philanthropist would be interested to give away 10,000 or so. There is something quite fascinating about pressing the button and seeing the numbers move up, so that this might be more effective than appears at first sight.

One ingenious suggestion from Jervis Smith was to use a piece of carbon paper and make a thumbnail imprint for each vulnerability.

I personally still favour the cards, as they cost nothing and can be used without anyone else seeing what is happening.

4.7 Group Discussion

The booklet was sent out without any discussion between myself and the recipients, to see how far they could take it from the booklet alone. However, the outcome showed that substantially better results were obtained when two or three of the experimenters got together and discussed it between themselves. Sidney Rosen suggests that a great deal of discussion is necessary before the unique significance of the vulnerability rate in determining the risks is fully realized.

It seems that it is not necessary for the discussion to be between experts. Two or three people, each having read the booklet, can get together, sharpen up their minds on each other and resolve the problems for each other.

The effectiveness of Discussion in breaking through mental barriers is now very well recognized in psychiatric circles, and at this point becomes of major importance in the proposals (derived from Sidney Rosen's and Dr. Adams' suggestions) made in Chapter 6.

4.8   Retention of the Idea

A good deal of evidence was received that once a motorist has caught on to this conception of observing his vulnerabilities it will stay with him ever after. This point occasioned much discussion because originally many people said that any kind of propaganda drive would be no good as it would need to be frequently repeated, and would gradually pall, anyway. The ultimate opinion is precisely the opposite. This is that once a motorist has been made aware of the idea, then every time he becomes vulnerable he notices it and is reminded to watch himself. This, if true, could be a particularly useful phenomenon (see also 7.2).

4.9   Ability of Drivers to Recognize their Vulnerabilities

Several experimenters had doubts as to people's ability to recognize their own mistakes. They objected to the booklet tying the thing down purely to the observer's judgement.

They are right as far as inexperienced drivers are concerned, beyond doubt. But it seems clear that there is an automatic education which takes place as one drives. Experience teaches. The close agreement between experienced drivers as to what is dangerous and what isn't, which I have observed everywhere, seems to indicate that at least the majority of people will conform to an accepted standard and will catch most of their own vulnerabilities.

It is clear that the ability to recognize vulnerabilities can be taught. Probably the best method is by discussion while driving. (See also 9.8.)

4.10   Interpretation of Results

The main deductions to be made are given below. They are much coloured by the many discussions which took place over the same period as the tests. A good deal of weight has been given to the 'hunch' of the men most closely in touch. These hunches are probably as significant as any measurement.

(i) It is clearly within the powers of any particular motorist, by counting his vulnerabilities, to reduce his chances of accident substantially; ultimately he can achieve some tenth of the average, i.e. to the point where on the average he will drive for 200–300 years per crash.

(ii) The conception of vulnerability rate, once implanted in the mind of a motorist, stays there and jogs his elbow every time he has any kind of narrow escape. It could be asked in what way this is different from any other idea implanted in a man's mind, such as fear of an accident or fear of the police. The answer is surely that the vulnerability idea stays there without any unpleasant associations or mental phenomena that would tend to suppress it. It is a constructive thing and a man remembers it as he might remember to collect his week's wages – because it's worth having – not as some uncomfortable, distressing idea, that he would like to forget.

(iii) It was not proved that distribution of a booklet alone, without other measures, is a suitable way of achieving results. The probability is that at least some follow-up is required.

(iv) A substantial improvement in traffic accidents could be achieved immediately by distributing a booklet and following it up by suitable propaganda. The sort of thing one visualizes is a campaign with a slogan 'Count your vulnerabilities'. Pessimistic interpretation of the results would suggest that about a 10% improvement in traffic accidents throughout the community could be counted on by this method. An optimist could easily make out a case for over 40% improvement. My own assessment is not much above 10%, though ways of improving this to perhaps 50% over a period (chiefly by group discussion) are considered in the following chapters.

As we have said, 10% is a high yield in this field. It makes a very good financial proposition, with an interest rate of 10,000% per annum on the expenditure. For example, in England such a drive could be set up for about £10,000 and could reach nearly all motorists for about £200,000. £10,000 is thought to be the minimum to overcome initial inertia. If the ultimate result is a 10% reduction of the £200 million per annum bill,* this is indeed 10,000% per annum interest on the investment.

In the United States the estimate of the National Safety Council (4th February, 1965) gives economic losses from traffic accidents at $8,200,000,000 – more than $1\frac{1}{4}$% of the national income. This means that a saving of at least 800 million dollars per annum (mostly by the Insurance Companies) is within easy reach.

* A quick check of this figure of £200 million in insurance circles indicates that it is almost certainly conservative.

CHAPTER 5

Applying Vulnerability Counts to Reduce Road Accidents

5.1 Action by the Individual

ANYONE who can get his vulnerability rate down to about one per day can expect to drive for 100 years or so per crash, and approximately 3,000 years per fatality. (The number of years is merely a vivid way of expressing the probabilities.) He will reduce his chances of serious injury once in his life time from about 1 in 4 (the average) to 1 in 20 or more.

Everyone who is not affected by some abnormal approach will feel that this is worth doing. It is, however, not at all easy. One may drive for a year without clocking up very many vulnerabilities. But a couple of really long drives, ending up perhaps with bad weather and bad road conditions, can cause one to ruin the whole year's record by incurring several hundred vulnerabilities in an hour or so. No one appears to have the slightest difficulty in recognizing when these extra vulnerabilities commence. Once the idea is in a motorist's mind, his attention is drawn to it as soon as he begins to take risks or to meet unforeseen happenings. The difficulty arises from the fact that he has no philosophy thought out in advance to cope with this situation.

What next he should do, as soon as he sees these dangers beginning to clock up, is to assess the cost of a crash compared with the cost of any alternative measures he can take to enable him to stop driving. To stop driving is often the only alternative (see 4.3). He should fix some arbitrary value on the price of a collision – say £1,000 or $5,000 – and then work out what measures he could take, with say half this money or less, to

59

enable him to stop driving until the next day, or until he is thoroughly rested.

The important thing to realize about this set of circumstances is that one is never in a good condition to think things out at the time. It has to be worked out in advance. Surely when one sees there is a possibility of excessive driving looming in the distance, that is the time to work these things out, and be prepared to face up to the alternatives.

It is illuminating to ask drivers for their estimate of the cost of a crash. They generally begin by saying no cost at all – the insurance company pays. Then they begin to remember that they often cannot recover the cost of hiring another car while their damaged one is being repaired; they begin to add in the losses if they are away from work for a week or two with some injury; and of course, the reality is often very much worse than this, with long-dated damage to health or goodwill or business relationships which is hard to assess. In fact, if one does assess such things the figures are generally too high to face up to.

Apart from the problem of abnormal vulnerabilities when tired, the procedure to cut down vulnerability rates is straightforward. The motorist should read the booklet and do the tests as described in 3.6. When he thinks he has a clear picture, he should get a casual acquaintance (never a wife or member of the family) to assess his vulnerability rate independently while they are driving together. If there is any discrepancy, the ensuing discussion will very quickly clarify the position.

The main difficulty in this is locating a passenger to make the long-drive check. But there is no hurry about it. Wait, if necessary, a year or more, for occasions when the right kind of person can join in a reasonably long journey. There is no need to feel that an accident is round the corner. On the average it is 20 years away, and the whole problem may be approached with a quiet mind.

Local road safety organizations could well offer a service of vulnerability observers on a volunteer basis to those drivers who would like to get themselves checked. This is, however, not an easy matter to organize and would require a good deal of administrative skill.

5.2 Action by the Authorities

The evidence presented in Chapter 4 may be sufficient for some authorities and agencies in this field to make a small scale move to encourage vulnerability measurements. The experimental results seem to show that a 10% reduction in accidents could be counted on.

All such authorities are bombarded by schemes with sensational claims of this kind. However specious these may sound, it is rarely possible to act on them. There is nearly always some hidden snag which the enthusiastic sponsor has failed to uncover. In the matter of traffic accidents it is particularly difficult to decide how to apportion the available money, because it is quite impossible to discover or prove whether a measure produces any result. What the statistics show is nearly always a matter of opinion (App. 5). The vulnerability rate scheme under these circumstances has much to recommend it. Firstly, it can be started on a very small scale. Secondly, it permits an indisputable measurement of results – as never before.

The way in which I think an authority or group of any kind should approach this is:

(*a*) Rewrite the booklet for vulnerability measurements (3.6) in terms of local idiom, eliminating anything which it is thought could offend local susceptibilities. One enemy will do more harm than a thousand friends can correct. (App. 12 gives an example of how the propositions may be cast in quite different language.)

(*b*) Make quite a small printing. Don't send the booklet out at random. Run a TV feature and other advertisements and only hand out the booklets to people who ask for them as a result of the propaganda. Make a small charge for the booklet. You are not after numbers, only interest. The small charge will eliminate the less interested.

(*c*) When you send a booklet tell the recipient that you want to hear how he gets on. Follow this up at three-monthly intervals with a request for the results. You can reasonably hope for at least a 20% yield over a year.

(*d*) From these replies it is easy to calculate quite accurately what sort of result has been achieved.

(*e*) If the results are successful, make a bigger printing and step up expenditure on propaganda. If the results are disappointing make minor changes in the basis of measurement. Suggest, for example, that observation be limited to the last hour on a long drive. Quite minor changes in approach are often sufficient to make the difference between acceptance and rejection and different communities react quite differently to certain phrases and expressions.

There is a limitation to what can be achieved by the foregoing method, which is fixed by the motorists' mind – the angry driver, the wild driver, etc. This residual group of accidents I call the hard core, and it is in tackling these that vulnerability measurements appear to find their most valuable application. This is considered in the following chapter.

CHAPTER 6

The Hard Core

WE have seen that there appears to be a hard core of accidents
that cannot be eliminated. This does not mean that there is a
hard core of motorists different from the others. The hard core
is a core of accidents, and the cause is the mental state, not of
some permanently wicked motorist, but of all motorists at some
time. (See Chapter 10 for a recapitulation of this.) The attitudes
producing these accidents seem to derive from over-assessment
of skill, from emotional involvement in the motor-car, from
being in a hurry, from anger, frustration, tiredness, boredom, a
buccaneering spirit, lack of social sense of obligation, from
intra- and extra-punitive compulsions; and similar moods.
These moods while they last produce a closed mind, and the
self restraints and disciplines which normally operate inside the
subject's mind are deprived of any power.

It is possible that ultimately an educational process may be
developed which, operating on the young, can prevent the
generation of this closed mind condition. This is considered
further in Chapter 9. No such process exists today, except by the
absorption of unconscious assumptions and social conventions
by the young from their surroundings. Clearly this process
already operates to quite a degree, but is not yet effective
enough to eliminate the hard core.

6.1 Intimidation and Persuasion

As we stand there is only one method available for keeping
this anti-social conduct in check. This is by the presence, or the
suspected presence, of the police, who can operate either by a
persuasive approach or by an intimidatory one.

The natural way to handle the more willing sections of the

public is by some means of persuasion. Many people for most of the time are doing their best and it would be a great pity not to keep them on side. Results, however, are generally disappointing. Even the best people at times are irresponsible or very hurried (Bib. 402) and a certain measure of intimidation is necessary to stop them going over the edge. Moreover, there is a decidedly sizeable section of the public that can only be prevented from driving selfishly and inconsiderately if there is some process of active discouragement all the time. These must be made to feel that they cannot disregard the community structure, its rules and regulations, without being made to suffer for it.

The problem then is, how to apply persuasion without being futile and how to provide intimidation without too much antagonizing. This is considered further in Chapter 11.

There is a very definite limit to the amount of discouragement or intimidation which can be brought to bear by the police, firstly because of cost and secondly because the police cannot get too tough with the public without reactions on their other work. There is a basic difficulty here that nearly all of us are potential criminals, as far as traffic crimes are concerned. The police must keep us in check as criminals one moment, but need our help and goodwill at another moment to deal with the very much smaller number of 'real' criminals. Is it any wonder that traffic offences are regarded today as much less of a social disgrace than other crimes? I am told in all countries that the respect and awe in which the police are held has much declined due to this, even to the point in England where young people will repeatedly disregard court summonses – an unheard-of thing fifty years ago. For these reasons, stepping up police pressure alone is no adequate way of making any inroad on the hard core.

Vulnerability measurement may give us an opportunity to use persuasive methods in tackling this problem, because it enables us to plant warning signals in the mind of the motorist which will operate in spite of a closed mind. This is because the warnings are factual, not emotional.

Let us consider this more closely. An angry man will refuse completely to listen to the voice in his mind that says, 'Be careful' or 'Stop, you are tired'. But he will still listen to the objective message, coloured by no emotions, received from his eyes that there is a truck blocking the road ahead. However angry, he puts on the brakes. If we can arrange for the information which his mind sends him about a vulnerability to arrive at his consciousness in this factual way, uncoloured by emotion, then he will accept this information and act on it, however strong the anger or other emotion dominating his mind.

This is a subtle point of great importance.* A truck hogging the road and making it difficult for him to get past sends an emotional message. He acts unwisely. The same truck blocking the road entirely sends only a factual message, involving no judgement and no balancing of conflicting emotions. He acts sensibly. He stops. (If on stopping he finds the truck is blocking the road unnecessarily and inconsiderately, the emotional colour returns and he may act without balance again.)

The information that he has incurred a vulnerability is uncoloured by emotion, apart from a possible, always mild, annoyance with himself. What emotion could there be? It is rather like finding he has left the traffic indicator operated. Only the bad neurotic could get upset by it.

A persuasive method of this kind is likely to be much cheaper than enforcement methods, more lasting in its effect on the mind, and could also help to reduce the almost intolerable burden on the police.

6.2 How can we Change an Adult Mind?

In order to make any inroads on this hard core of accidents by a persuasive method such as this, we must aspire to change the basic behaviour pattern under stress of the main body of drivers. This is generally regarded as almost impossible. Certainly only a programme extending over a good many years has a chance of success. Success in this area, however,

---

* This point may be clearer if one substitutes murder for vulnerability. A man may commit a murder in a state of high emotion. But the knowledge that he has committed it clearly cannot be wiped from his mind by the emotion. The fact is accepted, however bad the mental state, short of insanity.

is such a glittering prize that the objective must not be lightly abandoned. The reduction in accidents could be greater than by any other method.

There is little doubt that this problem will ultimately be solved, probably by a change in the unconscious assumptions of the community, and future generations will read of our traffic slaughter in the same mood of incredulity as we now read of other mass lunacies in history. Meanwhile, the question is whether we can make *all* ordinary motorists (not just the willing 10%) aware of the vulnerabilities which they incur. If we can, we will have given them an in-built warning signal* as to when their driving becomes dangerous.

The usual approach to this problem is to look for an acceptable motivation on which to base a propaganda drive. If a motive is found that appeals to all, then it is thought that enough money spent on plugging it will cause most people to respond. There are many such motivations, but none which look very promising. (See App. 8 for a more detailed analysis.) The most popular motivation used to be the frightfulness of bad accidents. Propaganda on this is now thought to produce some kind of emotional immunity. Such is the healthy reaction to all remote fears. It can't happen to us, we say, and in all probability, as we have seen, it won't. Success in implanting fear diminishes skill and increases accidents. Fear motivation ceases to operate, anyway, when a man becomes angry.

The most favoured motivation today is perhaps the creation of some kind of social convention. Jervis Smith puts it this way: 'Driving at high vulnerability is discourteous; the discourteous is ungentlemanly; if you are no gentleman no one will like you. In other words, try the body odour line to reinforce a change of conduct by a threat of ostracism.'

---

* Malfetti has suggested that an inbuilt warning signal might be obtained by electronic methods. A relationship can be established between an increase in carelessness and certain driving habits which can be detected electronically. (See Bib. 12 and 14.) Examples of this could be the degree of wander that a driver permits before his steering corrects it; or the way he grips the wheel. This leads to the possibility of a signal such as a flashing light appearing on the dashboard to warn the driver that his driving is becoming dangerous. This is a most exciting and promising line of approach, but still demands that the driver's mind be conditioned to accept the signal. Malfetti's remark quoted in Bib. No. 402 suggests that methods such as those advocated in 6.4 might still be needed.

A recent campaign (1964) in England using both fear and social convention was based on the slogan: 'Don't ask a man to drive and drink.' It had a remarkable success. It was possible to get a measure of this by counting the proportion of party occasions where it was mentioned. My score was an incredible 80%. However, this success is not typical of such drives. Firstly, the alcoholism drive was reinforced by some very subtle intimidatory activity, consisting of much-publicized experiments on trying drivers out to determine danger levels of alcohol in the breath. Secondly, it was operating in a field where the realities of the situation are already accepted.

No such general awareness of the situation, the causes of it and the cure, exists for the hard core. People not only don't know they are in error – they are profoundly convinced that they are not in error, that they know who is (some other fellow) and that they know what should be done about it (the pet theory, see Chapter 12).

6.3   The Knowery

We all possess a collection of things which we 'know', like this. 'Knowing' something is quite different from remembering it. We have a separate section in our mind where we store the results of all our experience of life. We winnow our experiences down to certain broad rules – often fearsome over-simplifications – and we use these to avoid the labour of thinking things out from scratch each time. We 'know' all kinds of things about our business – what works and what doesn't. Often these rules derive from one solitary happening years ago and are not generally true at all. We 'know' our wives, our friends, our children, are this or that – often a picture way off reality. We fix labels on people, whereas in reality all people are all things under different conditions (the most honest person is sometimes dishonest, the most dishonest sometimes keeps faith). We label Jews or Catholics or Protestants or Germans or Irish or Englishmen with some characteristic that fits in with these prejudices of ours.

For want of an accepted word, I call this collection which we prize so dearly – bought with so much pain and effort –

our 'knowery'. It is a magpie collection of material, very much like our 'memory', but with these extra emotional shades to it which make it very hard to change. Often the information in the 'knowery' is 40, 60 or even 80% poppycock. Perhaps 'prejudice' would be a better word.

This collection of near-trash which we carry around with us is one of the things that makes us old and unusable. Yet we resist anything which asks us even to take a look at it, let alone make a reassessment. We do this, too, with great passion. If we are pressed we tend to be angry, talk about a lifetime's experience, and dig in our heels worse than ever.

Embedded in this 'knowery' are all sorts of half-baked pre-conceived notions on driving motor-cars. Some of these are studied in more detail in Chapter 12 on pet theories. The question now is, how can we approach people to get a re-assessment of these notions?

Strangely enough, there is an answer. It is clearly not in lectures, not in comic strips, not in exhortations, not in ad-vertisements, not in meetings or rallies.

Is it perhaps in working through the artist? It is the artist who can affect our emotions and open our minds to new ideas. Wasn't it *Uncle Tom's Cabin*, and *Oliver Twist*, and so on, rather than the philosophers or philanthropists, that effected the great social changes of the last century?

Or is it perhaps via a suitable martyr? Was it Michael Collins rather than the Sinn Fein that stimulated Irish emotions to the point of the break-away?

I fear neither the artists nor the martyrs have very much of an opportunity in connection with traffic accidents. It is too small a subject, relatively speaking, for us to work up a state of high emotion. To do so would bring the whole thing out of perspective and wake up another basic instinct – not to make too much of an issue of things.

No, the answer is quite a dull and ordinary one, but very straightforward and easy to apply. It is to TALK ABOUT IT. The key to the closed mind lies in talk. Talk in small groups, ranging far and wide over the subject. Talk in an easy mood with no anxiety to reach a conclusion. Talk amongst friends, under pleasant, easy conditions.

One Shakespearean character says: 'I am a woman. If I would think I must talk.' And that goes – how it goes! – for all of us.

6.4 Group Discussions

This discovery of talk as a prophylactic is not new but its recent use has made immense strides possible in psychiatric work. 'Group therapy' is the label there. In some respects this is perhaps a more involved technique than the one we are now considering. But it is the same basic idea. Talk opens the mind. A man suddenly finds himself expounding something he didn't even know he believed, merely as part of an argument or because he saw a fallacy in what the other man said. The misunderstanding causes him to set out on an explanation directed at the other man, but it impinges just as definitely on his own mind. No one would ever convince him by talking at him. As Dale Carnegie says, no one ever yet won an argument. But lo! and behold! he convinces himself as a by-product of talking to or at other people.

Examples of this occur on all sides. For instance, one of the best techniques for getting a satisfied customer is to ask that customer to approach someone else on your behalf. The customer goes to see the other man, and talks in your favour, merely to convince the other man. But he convinces himself at the same time! And if you ever put a customer in the position that he has to talk against you to defend himself, you don't need to be told how quickly he convinces himself of everything bad about you.

Expounding on a subject in the face of mild challenge forces a man to mobilize his facts, straighten out his mind, and systematize his thinking.*

Summarizing, to change itself the mind must be made to think. Almost the only way to coax it to think is to make it talk – to 'think aloud'.

---

* Forcing a man to write a report is much used in administrative techniques to get the same effect – to tidy up the mind of the writer. It is useful, even if the report is never read by anyone afterwards.

To make this effective a good deal of bad temper has to be worked off first. There is such a lot of prejudice to come out! A lot of time is needed; a lot of patience; and a good many discussions over quite a period.

Exhort, or lecture, and with so much unreasonable emotion involved, you will inevitably only stimulate antagonism. Allow a man to explain his views to you, and talk himself out, and he may then, if left with it, accept a new idea.

6.5 Practical Measures

How can this be achieved on any worthwhile scale? There is a story of a defending general looking over a map and reaching forward with a black pencil to draw two long tracks across the country. 'That is how they will come,' he said. Another general leaned over, made a number of stars all over the map. 'No! That is how they will come,' he said, 'and how much more formidable that is going to be!'

This is what we need. We can only break this hard core by working in small groups, each initiating new small groups. We cannot do it by any mass movement, by any approach from large authorities. It has to come gradually, soaking into the community a man at a time. In other words, you and I must do it. What is the community? Just you and me over and over again.

Let me be quite specific. *You* must talk about traffic accidents. *You* must get two or three friends together and get them talking about vulnerability rates. Don't do all the talking. Get *them* talking! At least one of them will acquire a point of view. He will become motivated by his interest in the ideas, not by some selfish want. If you end up having motivated two people in this way you will have started a chain reaction (and with Uranium-235 as an example, there is no need to explain what that is).

Handling such a discussion is essentially an artificial activity – an acquired skill. It is quite different from dinner table conversation and different again from chairing political and business meetings. Bad temper should not be damped. The essential requirement is to let people talk themselves out. The essential equipment is a genuine and adequate knowledge of the subject, so that you can re-prime the discussion when it flags. (For which you should study Part II of this book.) The maximum number of participants is probably four.

You could perhaps start by stating quite baldly that you want to do something about traffic accidents, and believe that discussion about this vulnerability business is a good way. If only enough people will do it, you say, it might cut down accidents in a big way, and anyway it's a wonderful way of reducing your own risk. Get them together in your home, or in the corner of a club or a pub, and fertilize the conversation with this book or the little booklet (3.6) or anything else that comes to mind. Beyond that, obviously, it is a personal matter – each man to his own technique. You could perhaps consider buying several copies of this book, and lending them around.

How can you judge when the discussions have succeeded? I think by asking your man after a while whether he has begun to notice vulnerabilities without effort. If he has, and if the analyses in this chapter are correct, then your job is done. You have planted a seed and the rest will follow as the seed grows.

CHAPTER 7

Public Disinterest and How Vulnerability Counting Can Overcome It

CHAPTER 5 made some specific suggestions as to how an individual can reduce his risks of traffic accidents, and how any public authority can secure some worthwhile improvement in overall accidents by working through the more co-operative motorists. This group is small and the probable limit to the results achievable – 10% reduction – is fairly low. There was also outlined in Chapter 6 a method whereby a much more sensational improvement could be obtained – 50% or more – by the unorthodox method of fostering small discussions.

I have been at some pains to discuss the possibilities of this method with many friends who are experienced in public relations of this kind – politicians, social workers, church workers, rotarians, and so on. Without exception these conversations have been discouraging. Everyone concerned with trying to influence the general public is profoundly convinced of the enormous difficulty, if not impossibility, of getting any worthwhile response. There are tremendous resistive qualities. People are interested in their own personal lives, very busy making a living, and very tired at the end of the day. The better the quality of the man, the more completely he has got himself tied up and the less effort he has to spare for anyone else's baby. The poorer quality, who don't know how to fill in their time, are not interested, anyway.

7.1 Apathy

Short of an enormous publicity drive involving hundreds of thousands of pounds or dollars, nothing can triumph over public apathy, the experts say. 'Frightful, overwhelming apathy – not just to this but to anything!' Dozens of movements have asked people to make a small effort for good. Politicians, churchmen, social workers of all kinds, break their hearts and backs over it, but without result. All you get are the people who want to use it for social prominence, the cranks, and the compulsive 'do-gooder' looking for a chance to push somebody around and to restore some lost self-importance. There will be no result because the general public, not being afflicted with the spurious psychological motives, is not interested.

This may be one facet of what could well be the biggest sociological problem of the age – the suggestion that 'comfort plus security equals degeneration'. It is claimed that any community which sets security as its ideal must develop a selfishness and an apathy in the ordinary individual which will soon make him unreachable. All the best work in history, they say, has been done on the edge of the abyss. Strength and ability only grow under conditions which extend the powers a man already possesses to the full.

There seems little doubt that all this is largely true. Fortunately I am quite sure it does not apply to the motoring public. My friends are all completely wrong, in this case. In all the talks I have had about road accidents I have only met one person at any level in society who was apathetic over the accident problem. People may be a bit pathetic in some of their theories, but apathetic? Oh no! Fury, passion, violent convictions, a-plenty. No disinterest anywhere.

Perhaps the reason why there is so much interest in this subject is because motoring is itself so interesting – and often so irritating. There is a stimulus and a challenge to the driver all the time, as there is in any sport or activity with a slight element of danger. Or perhaps the explanation is that security can only ever come to those who are satisfied with the lower positions in the social scale. Those who want to rise to the top still have to fight to get there, and their tenure of the higher levels is always precarious, and dependent on their efforts. These people remain alive. These are the people who own cars. They aren't degenerate, they aren't apathetic, not even in the most welfare-ish state, and they are nearly all immensely interested in the accident problem, and very ready to do something about it. (They do little at the moment for good reasons – see Chapter 8.)

There are other more painful reasons why we do not meet the usual apathy in the motoring world. Too many people have lost loved ones, or have suffered serious trouble from road accidents. Great emotional energy is available here if it can be harnessed. Even those who haven't yet suffered a loss have seen or read of so many dreadful cases that it is far too close for them to remain untouched.

No, we may have our difficulties, but I am sure, in the face of the opinion of all the experts, that we will not meet apathy. If safety committees, rotary and similar clubs, church organizations and other such bodies will give it a start, it will reach the whole community within a few years.

7.2 Shirking

There is little doubt that we *will* have trouble with procrastination. We all put this sort of thing aside and never get round to it. If we do suddenly have an urge to do it we can't find the papers.

In this respect, however, the present plan has a strong edge on most sociological schemes. It contains an automatic daily nudge, plus a periodical sharp spike stuck in the victim, plus once in a while a most terrible clout over the head for him. An ideal set-up, this! – gentle reminders at regular intervals; a heavier one at longer intervals; and finally punishment for neglect! Once we have implanted the idea of vulnerability in a motorist's mind we have set all this working in him on our behalf. Every day he drives he will notice an odd vulnerability that will remind him that he should get down to working on this. Sooner or later – it may be after a few months, it may be a year or two – he will come up against a confrontation. The good sharp spike! He may still do nothing about it, but the reminder is vivid, and the daily nudges will be a little more clamorous after the narrow escape. If he still shirks, there will come other sharp digs from the spike and ultimately the terrible clout – the collision.

We will get procrastination, yes, and we must be patient. But we will get ultimate results beyond any doubt.

A very encouraging aspect of this also is that even if the resistance to the nudges and spikes is very high and a motorist never does anything specific about counting his vulnerabilities, or talking about the new ideas and spreading them, he will still more or less unconsciously be reducing his vulnerabilities all the time and giving us part of the effect we want.

7.3 Inability to Reason

Even so, say the experts, there still is very little hope of any results because even if people decide that they will co-operate they are on the average congenitally incapable of it. They don't have the thinking ability. They can't reason. There is no trouble that they will not accept, sooner than think. They can't study. They can't draw fine distinctions. They won't discern their vulnerabilities. Your book might as well be written in Greek.

I think there is a great deal of misunderstanding about this due to underestimation of the time that it takes many people to think. There is so much emphasis today on intelligence tests, mostly based on how quickly a person thinks, that we tend to lose sight of the more valuable qualities of character which enable a slow man to solve a problem just as effectively as a quick man, provided he has time.

We also fail to give enough weight to the effect of talking about these problems. Sooner or later things of this type get talked around – in pubs, over the lunch table, or at home with visitors or children. The thinking may take months or years rather than minutes. But it takes place ultimately.

We also greatly underestimate the difference between the positive and the negative moods in which a problem of thinking is approached. Precept, exhortation – in fact almost any form of teaching – induces a negative mood. What the mathematics master teaches most of us (through no fault of his own) is that we can't understand mathematics. What the literature master teaches us is that we don't like Shakespeare. But some children who can't remember a solitary lesson can give you such a mass of information about film stars, or aeroplanes, or pop singers, as passes all belief. They are often bottom of their class. One boy I know was bottom of his class at French until he spent a week-end at Calais. After that he was always top. He got into the positive mood.

People can co-operate I am sure, even the most humble of them, if they want to. Our problems boil down to making them want to – which can be achieved in time by planting in their minds an awareness of vulnerabilities.

PART II

The General Picture

In this section an attempt is made to give an outline of the general accident position, only so far as it affects the lay motorist. Many points of view, many important professional aspects, and many specialist activities have all been ignored or greatly simplified. The objective is to provide material for amateur discussions.

For those who would like to take it further, there are leads, in the form of references to the bibliography and appendices.

CHAPTER 8

Why the Public Won't Co-operate

HERE is a brief list of the main reasons why the public are not as co-operative as they might be in helping to reduce accidents.

8.1 No Motivation

Motorists won't co-operate in the first place because they don't want to. This is sometimes because the accident situation has failed to catch their sympathy. They feel that people only have accidents because they ask for them. Sometimes it is just a matter of selfishness, or lack of interest in the community. The most common explanation is probably the emotional complications which have been considered earlier in this book, particularly the fairy tales they tell themselves about their skill and their motor-cars; and the psychological satisfactions they get from their cars.

Most of the basic psychological motivations tend to put people out of sympathy with the problem. We do not appear to have a sufficiently powerful motivation to override these basic drives. This is elaborated in Appendix 8.

8.2 No Hope of Success

Many motorists feel there is nothing they can do to reduce accidents. Under these conditions the mind instinctively wipes the situation out of its consciousness. One knows instinctively that fervid resolutions to be more careful, which are only self-exhortations, are no more effective than any other exhortations. In fact, a sense of anxiety to do better in any matter of skill generally results in our doing worse.

8.3 No Lead

There is no consistent voice from authority. I asked nearly

everyone I visited what they would do, given unlimited powers, to reduce traffic accidents. The divergence in the answers was striking. Authority does not know at all what it thinks should be done, beyond what it is already doing. This is no reproach. The reproach would be there if it did know, and hadn't done anything about it.

All authorities must walk circumspectly in this matter, or more harm than good results. When some definite advice is issued, great care has to be exercised to placate the holders of the different pet theories, and to consider special interests. The valuable network of co-operation between all the authorities must be safeguarded. The result is mostly somewhat colourless and ineffective.

An outcome of this is to be seen from time to time in the press in the form of anguished letters from widows and heartbroken parents who have lost children. Almost always they contain a violent attack on some particular aspect that seems to the distressed person to be the cause of it all. (It never is of course.) None of this emotional energy is harnessed, because there is no clear lead.

A particularly vivid example of this situation appeared in one area early in 1965, as a result of an unusually bad year in 1964 regarding traffic deaths. The Government department concerned announced some new ideas to reduce accidents, primarily by introducing amateur road patrols. Over 20 other suggestions were made in a voluminous subsequent newspaper correspondence. A third of the suggestions were completely ineffective and the rest were all in the category of pet theories, which just might have had a vestigial effect. Had the Minister concerned been in a position to give an effective lead, he could have mobilized the strongest support to help him. He should have staged a drive on observing vulnerabilities.

8.4 Alibis

Because of the lack of realism on this subject, everyone has plenty of alibis. Pedestrians are the trouble; or women drivers; or slow drivers; or fast drivers; or the bad roads; or the unreasonably low speed limits which hold everybody up; or the

lack of speed control. Somebody – somebody else – should do
something!

8.5 Antagonisms

Many antagonisms are given a free rein on the roads. There is,
in many people's mental picture, a state of war between
pedestrians and motorists; between trucks and private cars;
between humble cars and big prosperous fellows; between cars
and motor-cycles, and so on. More general even than this is the
feeling of antagonism towards the wild driver. A careful driver
meets a case of really inconsiderate driving, and this makes him
angry. It is then a very easy step, which nearly all of us take,
to say – there goes the man who causes accidents. This is
certainly not always true (see 10.4a), but this does not reach the
mind of the man smarting under the bad conduct. He feels
both indignant and virtuous, and is in no mood to hear that he
himself, en masse, might well be as dangerous as the wild man
who has just passed. Nor does he see why he should be involved.
It is up to the authorities to catch and punish these objects of
antagonism.

Many bereaved people are searching, not for remedies, but
for revenge, and advocate quite preposterous measures.

8.6 Pet Theories

Most motorists have a pet theory about what should be done
concerning traffic accidents. They feel that until their pet
theory is adopted and carried out there is no point in trying to
do much else. They have never critically examined their theory,
never discussed it in relation to the larger issues, but it simply
never occurs to them for one minute that they could be other
than right.

This, of course, is an extremely fundamental aspect in the
sociological picture. Nearly every man has such a collection
of pet theories on politics, on religion, on how a family should
be run, on relationship between husband and wife, and so on.
He expounds these in the home and confirms them with his
cronies. It is nearly impossible to get him to reassess them.

There is nearly always some element of value in these pet theories, and very often it is by no means obvious why they would not succeed, or why they are not already adopted by the authorities. There is no hope of opening his mind to any new ideas while such a half-valid theory remains undemolished. Accordingly, the better known pet theories have been considered in a separate chapter (12) in some detail.

8.7 How can this Situation be Changed?

It will now be clear why the small discussion group is almost the only possible way of breaking down these barriers that prevent people from co-operating in any intelligent attempt to reduce accidents. In every case considered above a great deal of talk is necessary, directed at one particular individual, before he can be expected to reassess his views. Any general propaganda or general textbook would have to cover hundreds of different arguments, and no man can be expected to listen to all these if they don't impinge on his own views. Nor can he be expected to select the few that do impinge on his own views from any general propaganda. It has to be by individual conversation, in which he puts his points of view and this stimulates others to challenge it and add suitable facts to shake his convictions.

A good point of entry is to discuss the pet theories given in Chapter 12.

CHAPTER 9

Youth and Education

9.1 The Barbarian Invasion

A CONSIDERABLE proportion of young drivers are basically 'uncivilized' in their attitude.

An individual is 'civilized' when inhibitions have been created in his mind to produce behaviour patterns with which others can live. We are only able to live together at all because we have evolved some workable behaviour pattern towards each other. We learn to recognize the rights of others; we defer at doorways; we don't help ourselves to other people's property; we don't give way to all our angers. This behaviour is not natural. Each new generation is an invasion of barbarians, in whom most powerful inhibitions have to be induced before they can become either useful or happy. This civilization process is now somewhat hampered by pseudo-psychology, and other slacknesses, so that we find, for example, neighbours are increasingly inconsiderate, louts shoulder us off the pavement, the instinct to keep fit weakens, drug taking and other indulgencies become prevalent. A great increase in deviant behaviour appears, morally (delinquency), sexually (perversion), and culturally (no examples no quarrels).

Many motorists do co-operate with the authorities, but only when they think they may be observed and not because of any instinct that way. They may, perhaps, dislike or fear being caught by the police and all that that involves. But when they are sure that they can get away with it, they break speed limits, bully, attempt to teach other drivers a lesson, and generally commit endless acts of selfishness. They display remarkable cunning in escaping apprehension. This applies not only to the young men and the oaf, but to many older people who would permit themselves such conduct in no other sphere. The man

83

who instinctively defers to others in going through a door, or when out walking, appears to change his personality when he gets in a car. He does indeed *not* drive as he appears to live.

There is good reason to believe that 'civilizing' the young is achieved primarily by example; by virtue of the assumptions that we absorb unconsciously* from our environment. It is not what we are taught, but what is taken for granted by our teachers. Conscious teaching and precepts play a small role at best, and often even antagonize. To take an example, a man is kind perhaps because his mother was kind or because his mother took it for granted that he was kind; and not because a teacher said he ought to be kind. If he has been threatened too much with Hell Fire he may even acquire a certain compulsion to dare to sin.

Alexis Carrel in 'Man the Unknown', if I have him aright, says that to bring up a boy to be honest we should habitually throw at him an arbitrary imperative, 'Be honest!'; not embark on any persuasive approach.

This same folksy wisdom is enshrined in the old story of the father demanding to know the intentions of his daughter's boy friend. 'How do you mean?' says the youth. 'Well!' says the father, 'do you intend to marry her or what?' 'Gosh,' says the youth, 'do I have a choice?'

There is every reason to believe that we will not civilize barbarians or motorists by appeals to reason; only by tactics that produce the correct behaviour by means of an unconscious assumption or a habit that way.

9.2 Teaching Discipline

In the kindly Hertfordshire village where I grew up we often saw Mr. Connor's breaking-in cart driving around with a young and high-spirited horse in it. He would be fighting furiously against the restrictions of the harness and the weight of the cart. My father, who was very much aware of the slavery of the horse, explained it this way. 'The natural spirit of the

---

* Unconsciously, not subconsciously. This has nothing to do with the psychologists 'subconscious'. The subconscious may compel us to do things without our knowing why. Here we do things simply because we have never thought of doing anything else.

horse has to be broken,' he told me. 'The sense of joy in life of a young thing has to be turned into a hopeless acceptance of all indignities.' My distress at this picture remains with me today, and the very words 'breaking in' intimidate me.

Looking back I doubt whether this was a fair picture. He could have explained to me that a young horse needs to be trained and that he doesn't like his lessons any more than we liked ours. He might have said that if the young horse is not trained it damages itself, it stampedes, it can't usefully work; it is in fact much happier if it is properly trained.

The extreme kindness and the strong emotional reaction against cruelty which characterized the last few generations undoubtedly served to weaken some very essential disciplines. This was much reinforced by the advent of pseudo-psychology, which interpreted the new research on the emotional structure of the mind as indicating that young people must not be frustrated; that conflicts must not be set up; and so on. This of course is a gross perversion of the real discoveries. No sober psychologist has ever suggested that conflicts should not exist in a healthy mind. The truth is that without them and without a system of semi-automatic restraint there is no possibility of producing a social animal.

This is what we are now failing to do – to produce a social animal. Our youths are often like wild horses, extremely dangerous to those around them and also to themselves. It is interesting to observe too, that the kindness of the last few generations is replaced in these ill-disciplined young minds by a lust for cruelty which seems to know no bounds. One only has to see the flushed faces of the addicts coming away from an all-in wrestling contest to see how serious it is. They know quite well that this is not the real thing, but they enjoy it as their parents enjoyed a fairy play. Where their parents wanted sweet and happy endings and read novels which were gay and amusing, this new type looks for cruelty, morbidity and perversion for its delights. There can be no reasonable doubt that this is directly due to our failure to train or 'break in' the new Barbarians.

Perhaps the most astounding feature of today's picture is a tendency to say that the parents should provide the discipline. At no time in the history of the human race were the parents

expected to be the civilizing influence. As well expect the mare
to break in the foal. Parents are the last people we can ask to do
it, and it is to be hoped that no loving parent will be foolish
enough ever to fall for the stupid propaganda. If he does he
will see the fourteen or fifteen years of loving kindness he has
devoted to bringing the child to adolescence all destroyed and
turned into hatred, to no purpose. Not only will the child
often hate him all the more because of the previous kindness,
but at best he won't accept anything like the degree of unpleasant constraint and discipline from a parent that he would
from someone outside.

It is not the parents' *job*; but the failure may well be the
parents' *fault*. The people who are shirking the job – for very
good reasons – are the teachers and the employers. The reason
why the teachers fail is primarily because the parents won't
support them. Years ago if you clouted a boy for a misdemean-
our and his father happened to hear of it the boy got another
clout. Nowadays the father brings a legal action and supports
the child against the teacher. The reason why the employers
don't do it is that they can't afford to, and because the unions
are unreasonable over such matters. Thus sentimentality and
lack of proper firmness by parents, teachers, employers and
unions is, in the ultimate analysis, the real cause.

There is only one way to put this right. The disciplinary
bodies – the teachers and the employers – must do their job;
and the protective bodies – the parents and the unions – must
support them in this and drop the present sloppy attitude.

Perhaps it should also be emphasized that the barbarian
invasion will not be avoided by any 'proper bringing up' prior
to adolescence. If the adolescent is not wild he is not developing
healthily. 'Proper bringing up' will make it easier for him to
get through the wild period, but that is all. The taming process
can only start when the wildness appears, not in childhood.
This is the time when the instinct to break away from the home
also appears, and when parental authority is at its lowest.
The slightest word from a stranger has more influence than
anything the parent can say. Any adolescent who does not
show traces of this wildness has probably been overconditioned
as part of his upbringing. Of course, parents can make it harder

for him by failing to inculcate proper respect for authority or by unconsciously implanting an anti-social attitude. This is a problem beyond the range of this book. The present point is that their contribution is over long before adolescence. We shirk our responsibilities when we say that coping with adolescent wildnesses is the parents' job.

How does this affect the road accident position? At first sight one would wish to draw a distinction between the relatively small proportion of delinquent youths, and the much larger proportion (perhaps 20 or 30%) of quite decent well meaning young men who just have not been taught proper behaviour and who remain uncivilized. The delinquents are an unmitigated evil, and there is of course no solution except the most strong and determined action by the police and the courts. The larger well meaning group does ultimately get civilized – generally by the process of getting married and discovering that it must come to terms with the community to earn a living. It is often well on in life before this adjustment is made, sometimes into the 40s or 50s, and rarely before 30. From the point of traffic accidents there seems to be no distinction between the two groups. One is just as dangerous and produces just as much disaster as the other. One is just as unreachable as the other.

We can distinguish between these youths, who are uncivilized through and through, and the buccaneer adult who is civilized to a reasonable degree in his ordinary life, but who becomes uncivilized when he gets into a motor-car. This adult type we are perhaps justified in trying to reach, but we can hardly set out to civilize masses of youths with regard to their attitude to a motor-car, if their attitude to life as a whole is still barbarian. We can only hope to intimidate. If we do intimidate successfully, of course, we not only improve the road accident position; we also make a useful contribution towards their general 'breaking-in'.

Thus there can be no avoiding the conclusion that the police must adopt an intimidatory attitude towards youths who drive dangerously. All thoughts of 'sportsmanship' must be dropped. The matter is too serious. An example has to be made of everyone who is caught. If we don't knock it out of them while they are young, it may persist even into their 40s and 50s.

This does not mean that an era of bullying and unfair treatment has to be started. Great skill and understanding is needed to 'get tough' successfully: to distinguish between the wicked ones and the triers without skill. This is considered further in Chapter 11. What we are saying now is that the *trend* must be in the 'get tough' direction. The speed of progress can only be set by the availability of good quality men in the police and in the Courts, who will handle it intelligently, with the objective of bringing the youths ultimately on side.

I have told earlier of a case where a young barbarian was making hundreds of vulnerabilities a week and cut it down to a normal figure after what to him was a serious accident. I think most of us know of such cases. What we have to aim for is a situation in which *any* bad conduct or *any* quarrel with authority in any form produces an impact on these young people comparable with that of a serious accident.

No doubt this will offend many people, who are convinced that tolerance is a virtue. Tolerance is not always a virtue. Tolerance – if it implies toleration of evil – can be a very great vice. We must be very tolerant of the young man's ineptitude, but not of his lack of self-discipline.

9.3   Teaching Morality

Researchers in the field of traffic accidents are frequently impressed by the goodwill, freshness of mind and eagerness to learn that characterizes the young motorist. Spicer (Bib. 401) remarks on this, and on how amenable they are to instruction. This is not at all inconsistent with the barbarian qualities described in the previous section. Many a savage is very ready to learn, when his fancy is caught. Having learned he gives his selfishness and unawareness full rein.

Bad behaviour on the roads therefore is to some degree a moral problem. Courtesy, self-abnegation, a readiness to concede to others what they want, a readiness to accept bad behaviour from others without rancour – these are the kind of human qualities that help reduce traffic accidents.

Can these qualities be taught? Of course they can! Our whole civilization has evolved only because these principles

were, to some degree, successfully taught through the ages –
by the church, by philosophers, parents, loving aunts, loyal
servants, dedicated schoolteachers, and so on. The question then
becomes are we still succeeding in teaching these qualities today?
An attempt has been made to answer this in App. 9.

Some efforts have been made by the churches in recent
years to attack the road accident problem from the moral aspect
(Bib. 211) but they appear to have become discouraged.

Parents rarely teach morality applied to the roads, at least
not by example. In fact the parent who, in the hearing of his
children, curses the fools on the road as he drives, is probably
the rule rather than the exception.

My own observations are that those countries with the most
successful motorist education schemes (see next section) are
characterized by most bad temper on the roads. Years ago, in
the '30s, when I brought my Continental friends to England
they would gasp at the friendly deferment, the patience and the
good temper of the motoring fraternity generally. The English
motorists were literally a fraternity then, so different from the
Continental antagonisms, with their furious 'Chameaux' and
'Saucissons', and general 'bluff-him-off-it' approach. Now
nearly every Englishman seems to know most beautifully and
exactly what is expected of him, but, goodness! How sternly he
expects it from others! How ready he is to hoot, reprove, and
hurl abuse if his own particular set of shibboleths is desecrated!

The conclusion is that technical education needs a moral
backing to yield its full benefits.

How this is to be done in our modern society is perhaps a
good subject for one of the discussions I have been advocating.
My own view is that it can only be spread by the discussions
themselves. One could begin such a discussion by examining
two unconscious assumptions, the prevalence of which indicates some inadequacy in our civilizing process:

    1. That a man has a right to take what the law allows him
(the point being that the law is an imperfect working rule,
not a licence).

    2. That a man has a right to become indignant and angry
if someone else misbehaves. (Which he has not.)

9.4   Teaching Traffic Tactics

Educational work is being done in all countries to prepare the young for entering the traffic maelstrom. It is an essential part of what I have called the professional safety structure, described in Section 10.1. Without these educational activities the field for the new ideas in this book would not exist. At least two excellent manuals for teachers are available (Bib. 216, 217).

The educational problem is a most unusual one, and should be approached with diffidence. One gets the impression that it calls for teaching methods radically different from any other subject. The following tentative remarks are offered only to fertilize discussions.

It would appear that there are only some thirty or forty rather simple rules or ideas that can usefully be formulated. One part of the problem is to incorporate these in the minds of all motorists so that they are always acted upon in times of stress, of inattention, of distraction, and so on. For complete success each of the ideas should be called up and utilized correctly on every single occasion it is needed. This is not in the least like teaching a school subject. It is more like teaching a concert pianist, who must never hit one single solitary wrong note. Moreover, the objective is that all pupils, not just the promising ones, but the most stupid and inept, must be brought to this level of perfection.

As an example of the resistance of the general public to this, one may take the conception of minimum stopping distance, dependent upon response time of the driver, braking efficiency of the vehicle, and speed. The maximum efforts of the educational groups in most countries have been put on to this concept for years. Has it reached the reader? Can he say what is the accepted minimum stopping distance at 30, 40 and 50 m.p.h.? And can he judge these distances correctly? He will be a most exceptional case if he can.*

---

* The minimum distances frequently quoted are 25, 40 and 58 yards respectively. These appear on the back cover of the 1964 Highway Code – probably the most prominent spot in England for this kind of information. (See App. 10 for a further examination of this.)

The foregoing does not mean that the propaganda campaign failed. The objective may well have been only to implant the realization that the distance is greater than would be expected. The mental resistance to recording three simple figures is, however, clearly demonstrated.

The technique most favoured for this kind of teaching is that of constant reiteration, first from one angle then another. The difficulty is to attract and to retain attention. Everyone feels he has mastered the point long before he has fully incorporated it into his automatic procedures. Many ingenious devices and many remarkable films have been produced, aimed at capturing attention and reiterating the essential points. Unfortunately I have not located any co-ordinated distribution centre to which I can refer the reader for details. An impressive collection of machines and films can be seen at Rospa House, 17 Knightsbridge, London, S.W.1 (see Bib. 205), and, I am told, with the Aegis Insurance Co. in New York.

As to what these 30-odd vital points are, the bibliography gives some references under 'Teaching'. Attention is drawn to Bib. 202 which represents Rospa's views, after much teaching experience, as to the precise matter to be taught. It is interesting to compare this with the more comprehensive information used by police instructors for their own drivers (Bib. 201) in England, and with the textbooks used in U.S.A. and Australia (Bib. 216 and 217). Educational procedures for school children, tenderfoot motorists and driving instructors have been the subject of an immense amount of study and experiment in the U.S.A. This has been much encouraged by research grants (Bib. 21) and by the farsighted policy of the Insurance Companies in granting rebates to holders of school diplomas in driving techniques, and to certain other categories of young people.

Much success has been achieved in teaching other special groups besides police drivers. An account of some experiments is given in Bib. 1, pp. 134–7. Groups of professional drivers, whose living depends on co-operating with the boss, are naturally more receptive to indications of required procedures than the general public, so that one cannot deduce any very definite conclusions from these results. In fact, it does not follow that the improved results justify the procedures at all. Any member of a team anxious to turn in a good accident-free record, and aware that he will suffer adverse prominence if he fails, will inevitably pay much more attention to his driving than usual. This will reduce his vulnerabilities and therefore his accidents, even if the only procedure inculcated were to twirl a rabbit's foot.

This uncertainty should not be interpreted as any antagonism towards education. I asked Dr. Smeed why he had not included education amongst the measures studied in his overall review (Bib. 3 and 10.1). He replied that he restricted consideration to those methods, for the effectiveness of which there is some valid evidence. For further educational processes we have not as yet the necessary evidence.

9.5   Teaching Mechanical Knowledge

It is generally agreed that it is worthwhile to teach mechanical knowledge of a car wherever possible. It is thought that understanding his vehicle, and taking pride in it, contributes to greater care being taken by the driver.

It would seem unwise to combine this kind of training with any of the foregoing, as it cannot be expected to appeal to all motorists. The method of teaching is also quite different. This is orthodox technical training, the methods for which are well established and differ completely from the indoctrination techniques referred to in the previous section.

9.6   Teaching Skill in Handling Vehicles

Skill in traffic tactics, i.e. in deciding what to do, is quite different from skill in doing it, i.e. in handling the vehicle. Quite different teaching methods are called for. The problem of handling a vehicle is akin to tennis or golf or any other activity combining physical and mental skills. The learning procedure is largely a matter of teaching oneself. It consists in rehearsing certain movements or procedures or thought sequences over and over again, so that they become available for instantaneous automatic use when required.*

---

* It is perhaps not generally realized that these movements and thought sequences can be practised almost as successfully in the imagination, say while in bed, as on the tennis court or on the roads. (See App. 10.)

The function of the teacher in this process is primarily to stand by while the pupil fights the battles with himself and to step in when he gets into trouble, to save him from any calamity. Success in teaching this type of skill therefore is primarily success in self-effacement. Occasionally the teacher succeeds in analysing some difficulty, and showing the pupil a better method or a trick of the trade. The best performers are rarely good teachers.

The difficulty in developing this type of education lies in locating suitable teachers. The wrong teacher can so easily induce anxiety and defeatism, even to the point of moving final success out of reach for life. The big argument about teaching these skills therefore is whether the harm is more than the good. They can be learned without a teacher, and it could be that the money and effort available should go to producing suitable practice grounds, very fully equipped so that young men can take their vehicles there when they first get them, and practise stops, turns, skids, etc., until they are competent to venture on to the roads. Such a ground would presumably develop friendships and become a community centre of sorts, so that one could count on the young people learning from each other (which does not involve as big a risk of discouragement as with a formal teacher).

This problem has been tackled very successfully in England by using the motor-cyclist clubs (Bib. 210). Large proportions of young people graduate to a car by way of a motor-cycle and the clubs are very popular. All the different teaching techniques described have been incorporated in one course. Many practice grounds have been made available under this and other schemes in England, mostly from local government sources.

There is probably great scope at the moment, for anyone minded to make a practical contribution, for inventing suitable equipment and suitable techniques for improving such practice grounds. One could visualize a situation developing ultimately in which such grounds are used in examinations for licences, and come partly under control of the licensing authorities.

This could also be a method of teaching another skill, which at the moment appears to be overlooked. This is a very significant skill, and can mean the difference between life and death.

I refer to the technique of handling a car going out of control at high speed. A careful driver may well drive for most of his life without once meeting this situation, and only discover in his middle or late years that he has no notion whatever as to how a car behaves, or what he should do with it, under emergency conditions. However, this is a very difficult subject and much research still needs to be done. One airline trying years ago to teach pilots what to do when an engine failed on take-off was said to have broken up more aircraft teaching than they ever would have done in service.

9.7 Instruction Behind-the-Wheel

To produce a safe driver we must be sure that at no stage will any damage be done to his self-confidence. It is imperative therefore that the terrors of the traffic should not be loosed on a beginner until he is at ease in handling the vehicle. Nor must he be allowed to live with doubts about his ability to handle the vehicle over a long period, as so many parents achieve by allowing their children to have odd short spells at the wheel when opportunity offers. The only thing this teaches them is that they are unsure as to whether they will be able to handle the car, and this lesson remains with them throughout life.

The child should never be allowed to touch the wheel until he is old enough to apply for a licence. Then he should practise handling the car off the roads for an hour a day every day until he is completely at ease. Then he should have a few days on the roads, at least an hour a day, followed by one or two really long drives. This should be followed immediately by the licence tests; then out alone every day for at least a month.

A car with automatic clutch and gears is an enormous advantage over this period, by postponing a difficult aspect until complete ease and confidence in other respects can be brought to it. Stalling a car conspicuously in heavy traffic can unnerve even an experienced driver and can do semi-permanent damage to a beginner.

Behind-the-wheel instruction, as carried out by motorist schools and various authorities, seems to consist of instruction partly on road tactics and partly on handling the vehicle. We have seen (9.4 and 9.6) that these two facets of the problem require totally different methods of teaching. One wonders whether it is possible to combine them in one instructor.

There is much preoccupation with this problem of the instructor everywhere. Everyone feels that there should be a careful instruction course for the instructor. Frequently registration of instructors is advocated. An elaborate investigation of driving instruction using the technique of 'critical incidents' is described in Bib. 208. This has led to a technique of checking and grading teachers (Bib. 215).

9.8   Teaching Versus Persuading to Think

It is necessary to recognize that a number of different learning procedures* exist in the mind. Some learning consists in the adoption by the mind of a mode of reasoning which is recognized as inherently sound. Other learning consists of committing certain ideas, or sequences of ideas, to memory – so-called learning by rote. Mathematics, for example, can be learned in either of these two totally different ways. The student who learns to think in mathematical terms has acquired a much more valuable skill than the student who has merely learnt off the formulae and the sequences of steps leading to them. It is illuminating to observe the two types of mind in the process of recapitulation in preparation for an exam. There is no difficulty in recognizing which is which.

Learning unconnected facts such as in anatomy, or useful data such as trigonometrical formulae, has to be by rote. But if the underlying techniques are also learned by rote the result is an awed and intimidated mind, and often a dead mind, unable to apply what it knows to new problems. Much teaching for examinations achieves only this. When instead the student incorporates the lines of reasoning into his mind, using the teaching or the text books more or less as sign-posts to his own thinking, then he brings a constructive and uninhibited approach to any new problem.

*This bears little relation to the so-called 'learning theory' as used by psychologists in relation to the formation of emotional structures derived from experiences.

Similarly, in mastering driving one certainly needs to know all the correct procedures as taught by the methods which we have been considering above. None of this, however, bears much relation to the observation of vulnerabilities. It is quite a separate problem, requiring a totally different technique, to get a driver actively to observe himself and lift his awareness of what he is doing, i.e. to give him a free mind which is master of the situation.

This is why it is so important that the assessment of vulnerabilities be referred back to his judgement. In the small booklet (3.6) there is no reference whatever as to what the vulnerabilities are. He must decide. To give a list of possible vulnerabilities, or to attempt to combine the propaganda with any of the present methods would defeat the objective.

This presents a great problem in dealing with the more docile type of person, who wants to be told exactly what to do. He can get very annoyed and even distressed when told to work it out for himself. Yet the success of the operation depends entirely on his doing just that. It was therefore with much reluctance that I yielded to many requests by including App. 15 in this book. I did it because many people did need a few examples to see clearly what was meant by the term vulnerabilities. I have however, made it incomplete and provocative so that few will read it without wanting to change it.

The effect of persuading a driver to think about vulnerabilities does not stop with the resultant changes which he may make in his traffic tactics. The effect that we are looking for is that he will become more aware of the problems and more alert. This will make him safer, irrespective of traffic tactics or any specific practices he may adopt.

9.9 Teaching Visual Perception

We have seen in Chapter 2 that the quality in a driver most capable of improving his vulnerability rate is that of adequate visual perception, by which we mean not only what he sees but what he deduces in his mind from it – mental awareness derived from seeing. Such a quality is not much use unless one presupposes that the driver has skill in handling his car; has ability to judge distances and speeds; pays attention to the rules; gives the right signals; and generally co-operates. If a driver has this primary equipment, then the ultimate risk of accidents becomes determined as we have seen in Chapter 2, largely by this quality of visual perception.

People with this well-developed visual perception often know at once precisely what kind of person is driving the car in front of them or behind them, and what he can be expected to do. They see glimpses of pedestrians behind obstacles or reflected in windows. They see oncoming cars between trees on a distant stretch of the road. They sense a child's playground by the most elusive signs long before they come to it. They see the sort of house from which a child could suddenly dart out. They see reflections, shadows, water tracks, cart droppings, old skid marks. They feel how wind and water and light impinge on the whole landscape, so that they know when to expect a bad patch of road. They feel what kind of people come out from what kind of building or opening. They are aware of school hours, market habits, shopping trends, theatre traffic, drinking hours, and so on.

Perhaps the most remarkable quality in those with good visual perception is ability to see what movements are to be expected from all the mobile items appearing in the picture ahead. This particular quality is sometimes seen demonstrated sensationally on a football field. A player seems to know just how everyone else on the field is going to move in the following few seconds. He sees them not only as they are, but as they will be. He creates this picture of the future for himself by an amazing mental co-ordination of innumerable pieces of knowledge, instincts, feelings and guesses. Good drivers do the same.

This ultimate skill is clearly not something easily taught. In fact trying to teach it could well inhibit its development. It is a product of continued interest and attention over years, with the mind and body constantly working away, trying to get more and more master of the situation. It comes, like all other top achievements, only to those who are so interested and dedicated that they keep at it year after year. Most drivers do this without being aware of it.

There is no doubt that certain elements of visual perception are imparted during ordinary training and by ordinary conversation. Some of the simpler tricks like watching shadows are easily taught. If the method of development is as suggested above, chiefly by experience, there is clearly a limit to the amount that can be taught. The questions as to whether there is any way to be found for speeding up the learning of this quality, or for making young people aware of its importance, form obvious stimulation points for good discussions. One point of view is that making the young person aware of the need for it is already the greater part of the job done.

9.10 Dangers of Incorrect or Unskilful Teaching. The Positive Mood

In teaching there is a basic principle – choose the right time. If possible let the student take the initiative and let him ask for it when he's ready. He will then learn unbelievably quickly. Try too soon, or leave it too long, not only is it much, much slower, but much harder for him. Moreover, the proficiency achieved is never so high. Anyone who has trained a dog knows this. The Dalton System recognizes it in school planning. Most school systems violate it abominably.

As an illustration of this a friend of mine left school at 13. At 17 he knew no foreign languages, or mathematics or science or literature. Yet still at 17, in the positive mood, after three months of intensive study, he caught up with his fellows who had stayed at school for those four years, passed the same exam as they did, and went on three months later to take a top university scholarship.

Can we use this in teaching the young to drive? Or is the subject comparable with teaching an air pilot, i.e. something that has to be done immensely thoroughly and carefully. Do we tend to make too heavy weather of it because the accidents are making us over-anxious?

Certainly there is rarely any need to teach young people the mechanics of handling a car once they own one. They teach themselves within a few hours of its arrival. Try instead to teach them with odd tries on someone else's car and many will remain unhandy even for years. Or leave it until they are

middle-aged and they are condemned to the agonized motoring
school jerkeries that we see in back streets.

What young people learn in this positive mood stays with
them for life and becomes completely automatic. For example,
if such a driver wants to stop he stops, just as, if he wants to
raise his arm, he raises it. There are no intermediate conscious
processes. A late or over-anxious learner has to think about it.
'Let me see,' his mind says, 'I want to stop. I must put on the
brake and press down the clutch pedal.' Then – only then – he
stops. This point is elaborated in Appendix 10.

These doubts concerning educational methods are perhaps
worth listing, as possible material for discussion groups:

(1) By waiting for the right moment much teaching may
be avoided. If we force it when the subject is not in the mood
for it we may create a distaste for the lessons, and an immunity to later appeals. (How many people would have
enjoyed playing the piano, but for the miseries of some
teaching procedures?)

(2) We can make too much of an issue of things and produce a state of over-anxiety.

(3) We can complicate things unnecessarily, and bring
many things into consciousness which normally would be
taken in one's stride.

(4) We may make the student try too hard, which invariably produces deterioration in skill (Bib. 303).

(5) We may inhibit the growth of automatic response and
create a semi-permanent two-stage thought process (see
above and Appendix 10).

(6) We may induce the negative mood (by which I mean
that defeatist associations develop in the mind).

(7) We may inhibit the operation of intelligence, so that
people drive to rule, even when it is not sensible to do so.

(8) We may create an immunity to certain ideas. (I believe
the Webbs at one stage endeavoured to sell Fabian ideas by
incorporating them in training schemes and examination
questions at school. It was found to induce a feeling of dislike

for the subject and an antagonism towards it that alienated the victims for life.*)

(9) By putting too much emphasis on rule we can induce a mood of exaggerated righteousness, resulting often in quarrelsomeness and bad temper or in attempts to push others around.

(10) By putting too much attention on rules we may distract from, or diminish the importance of, the more fundamental techniques such as the development of visual perception.

9.11 Teaching an Attitude of Mind

It was suggested in Chapter 2 that the unrealistic attitude of most motorists to their car and their driving is the overriding cause of accidents. All investigators sooner or later seem to arrive at this point. If the attitudes were sound, no disciplinary effort, either from within or without, would be needed.

The best way to teach an attitude of mind is indubitably for the whole community to take it for granted. (Compare App. 9.) The question then arises, why should we not make a teaching effort to persuade parents and schools to create such an atmosphere.

It is also possible to explain to young people how certain emotions will develop in the future, in such a way that when the time comes they recognize the phenomenon and are better equipped to cope with it. (Bib. 225.) It seems, therefore, quite possible that young people could be warned about the car fever before they catch it, and learn to recognize it. This might well be a most successful prophylactic.

Let us try to visualize the sort of thing that might be said, not by the regular school teacher but by an outside visitor, say from the Parents' Association. This could be on an unusual occasion, associated in their minds with a break from school routine. The ideal set-up might be for a full day's break from ordinary work,

---

* This information was given to me by a mathematics teacher when I asked him to work out a few probability calculations which could be included in school syllabuses, to give the boys a picture of the probability structure described in Chapter 2. He advised strongly against it.

to be devoted to a visit from the accident circus (Bib. 205) with lectures, perhaps a play, and an open invitation to parents and friends. Such a set-up would make a deep impression on young minds. The vital thing is that it should be a substitute for school work, a tremendous beanfeast, a day of fun; not an additional load after hours.

The sort of thing that might be explained to the children would be:

(i) A motor-car is only a device for getting from one point to another. Not an adventure or a pleasure in itself.

(ii) Having a powerful or luxurious motor-car does not make you appear more powerful or more attractive, except to very foolish, undesirable people.

(iii) Girls do not judge boys by their motor-cars but by themselves. Those who see it otherwise are not worth bothering about.

(iv) Sports with a slight element of danger, such as ski-ing, gliding, sailing, are a great joy and an intelligent activity. They are just as satisfying as motoring and much more valuable in what they do to you. Moreover, you do not push the risks on to others as you do by show-off driving.

Teachers and parents would be asked to attend a separate lecture on confirming this attitude by implication in all they did. They would be asked to make sure that when they were out driving their behaviour supported it; not to try to buy unfair ascendancy for their children by giving them expensive motor-cars; and so on.

There would be opportunities on such an occasion for discussion groups between parents, teachers and children – not large discussion groups with most participants only listening, but little groups of four and five gathered round a lunch or tea table.

Safety stunts could be staged such as dropping a dummy (see App. 4), measuring response times (App. 1), and so on.

There would be an opportunity for parents to get familiar with the school safety library – which every school should have.

It might be a splendid occasion to put on a short play, and

if the play were in the grounds of the school, even to introduce a real motor-car or so. A film such as 'Six Candles' could be screened.*

This kind of activity would be most rewarding to a group of retired men. They could take it at their own pace, to as many or few schools as their resources allowed. They could devote weeks or months to preparation for their big day. They could invite newspapers, local V.I.P.'s, Rotary Clubs, etc., to participate and generally have themselves a whale of a time!

*Most Safety Organizations have a library of such films.

CHAPTER 10

What Causes the Accidents? What Can Be Done?

THERE are few accidents due to a single cause. Probably most serious accidents involve four or five things going wrong one after the other or all together. Any attempt to pick out some one cause as the villain takes on the colour of a pet theory.

An attempt to allot weight to the different causes is given in 12.12 but only by way of example. An estimate of the effects of various preventive measures (quite a different thing from causes) is given in 10.1 below.

This question of the relative value of the different measures is not as significant as might be thought. Wherever there is promise of improvement it is worth having a go to get it. Discussing the relative importance is rather like discussing whether one gets 1,000 or 5,000% dividend. It is all worthwhile. This seems to be fully appreciated by the authorities in all countries in a truly remarkable way. If there is any promise of improvement they have a go to get it.

10.1 Basic Factors. The Professional Approach

I have told in Chapters 3 and 4 of many discussions with authorities in U.S.A., U.K. and Europe. In addition, everyone who came my way – cab-drivers, visitors, odd acquaintances in the street – were bedevilled to the limit. The main aim was to get views from all angles on the road accident problem; and especially to collect 'hunches' as to what are the most effective measures to reduce accidents. The vulnerability rate idea often came out during these discussions, but mostly as an incidental.

I discovered that the situation differed vastly in different communities. Certain hunches, such as the big influence of

alcohol and of speed are widely held. Others, equally strongly
espoused, are purely local. For instance, in Los Angeles and
New York the major resentment is against lane changers; in
London, against the slow drivers; and in France against the
sin of 'doubler' which I understand as unwise overtaking. No
one with whom I spoke in these cities failed to raise the particular local bugbear, often with passion.

The probability picture also differs widely in different cities.
Pro rata, Los Angeles apprehends double the number of
violations of traffic law that London does; New South Wales
kills twice as many people as New York, London or Paris.
In London 40% of collisions involve pedestrians; in Los Angeles
only 10% – yet the number of pedestrians killed is about the
same in both cities (all *pro rata*).

Practices differ equally widely. In Hawaii, licences are
granted to youths of 16, who then proceed to kill about three
times as many people as youths of 17. In England a man can go
out drunk and kill two people and be fined £25; and so on.
In Los Angeles it is said that a man can be apprehended for
leaning up against his car while drunk, on the assumption
that he might be about to drive; also in London.

In spite of these divergencies, a completely coherent picture
emerges of what can be done – and is being done – to reduce
accidents. This picture is almost entirely in terms of action by
professionals – the police, the educators and the traffic planners.*
All else is secondary. Accidents happen because motorists make
mistakes. Only the police and the educators can provide the
discipline required. Only the traffic planners can make it
easier to avoid mistakes.

By comparison with these factors, all amateur attempts to
work on the motorists' minds are a poor bet. They are not
useless and certainly not to be decried. This book is directed
towards advocating another such attempt. *But*, by comparison
with what the police and the traffic planners can achieve, we
must recognize the relatively small yield to be hoped for.
Moreover, this is only within reach if the professionals take it

---

* The term traffic planners is intended to include all those working on traffic
flow, signs and signals, road engineering, traffic separation, traffic regulation and
so on.

up (see App. 6). Were I the man holding the purse strings, I would spend all the money on the three E's – Enforcement, Education, Engineering – through the professional channels, and using the orthodox methods.

The most powerful way to reduce traffic accidents, therefore, is to work on dull and thankless detail, as is being done now by the police and by all the associated authorities, research institutions and other organizations.* In each community a thousand special individual problems arise. These are such things as road surfaces, signs, traffic regulation, car equipment, configuration of crossings, separation of traffic flow, separation of pedestrians, methods to avoid frustration from delays (i.e. to keep traffic flowing), public relations (both by persuasion and by intimidation), regulations, court procedures, the structure of the law, procedural practices towards offenders. In each community, the many authorities and the public work together as a team to build a complex social structure that works magnificently. Every year, they improve it a little – eliminate a danger spot here, modify some practice there, and so on.

The way it all interworks is quite surprisingly different in different communities. In any one place everyone understands the signals, what is expected of him, and what to do. But what is right for one area is completely wrong in another. The motorist coming from one to another is often bewildered. As the structures grow in complexity, so the divergencies deepen, and work done in one area is of ever-diminishing value in another. For example, the thirty-seven references quoted by Dr. Spicer (Bib. 401) and the forty-eight quoted by the British Research on Road Safety textbook (Bib. 1) with reference to driver characteristics, contain only three references in common. However, an International Road Safety Congress now takes place annually (Bib. 106), and there are many signs of a move towards co-ordination.

The success achieved in each community is staggering, and the talk about mounting road accidents, although perhaps

---

* One of the largest research centres in America, the Transportation Centre at North-Western University, is orientated to work almost entirely for or through the police (Bib. 4).

effective from the propaganda point of view, is not a fair picture of the position. For example, in England there has been an effective reduction of traffic accidents between 1935 and 1965 of 90% (see Chapter 1). This is the summation of an enormous and continuous effort. Any stunt which distracts attention from it, or propaganda which decries it, is surely to be discouraged.

There has recently appeared (Bib. 3) a study by Dr. Smeed of the Road Research Laboratory in England, indicating what improvement still lies in reach there by different types of what might be termed 'professional' activity. This may be summarized thus:

	Per cent. Reduction in Total Casualties or Injury Accidents
Vehicles	
Replacement of all motor-cycles and bicycles by cars ..	34
Safety Helmets for all motor-cyclists	5
(19% in motor-cyclist casualties.) ..	
Safety helmets for all pedal cyclists	4
(33% improvement in cyclist casualties.)	
Use of anti-locking brake devices by all cars and commercial vehicles..	3
Use of safety harness by all car occupants	15
(See, however, comments in 10.7.)	
Road Engineering	
More street lighting	2
Surface treatment of accident black spots to reduce skidding	2
(80% reduction in wet road skidding accidents.)	
Building by-passes already planned	4
Building motorways (freeways) already planned ..	3½
Improving black spot junctions by traffic signals, roundabouts, staggering of crossroads, etc.	2
(Reduction at a particular junction can often be 40% or more.)	
Road Usage	
Increasing police by 10%, all used for patrols ..	25
Prevention of driving after drinking	5
Reduced parking on roads	10
Speed limits on all roads	5

The percentages cannot be directly added up, but an overall improvement in England of 60 to 75% is thought to be possible. A quick check indicates that there is less gold left in the ground in U.S.A. and probably a good deal more in Australia.

10.2   The Automatic Pilot. Inattention

Most of the work handled by the human brain is done without any reference to the conscious part. All our lives we work away pushing more and more on to this magnificent computer. (See App. 10 for a slight elaboration of this theme.) To take one simple example, at one stage in life it takes enormous concentration and much effort to tie a shoelace. Later we do it automatically without a thought. The complex movements of a tennis racket hitting a top spin volley are produced, after much practice, automatically almost as a reflex, in a fraction of a second.

Most actions involved in driving are handled in the same way. As we get more experienced we are able to hand over more and more to a kind of automatic pilot in our minds. Ultimately on a regular drive to the office, for example, we can spend the whole of the time thinking about the morning's task, and do not even know we have been driving at all. When we move house we nearly all have the experience of arriving, under automatic pilot, at the door of the old home.

This automatic equipment which we develop in our minds is provided with the most gratifying recall system, whereby the occurrence of any abnormality causes it quickly to call in the conscious part of our minds to take over. Our attention is attracted by almost anything abnormal, but *only* by the abnormal.

Anyone who drives regularly will recognize all this, and be able to fill in supplementary detail.

This denizen of the roads has been rather neglected in studying traffic accidents. He complicates the issue quite a bit. For example, the answer to the question of who has the most accidents is easily given. It is the automatic pilot. This you can check, because each vulnerability is an abnormality and the pilot calls you in. You can count them therefore, when you are on automatic pilot, just as when you are consciously attending to your driving. Try this after you have got into the habit of observing vulnerabilities, and you will find that most of your vulnerabilities are incurred by the automatic pilot. (It is not easy to try this, because you can't hand over to the automatic pilot just when you want to. The process is rather like going to sleep. If you try to make it happen too anxiously it won't have anything to do with you.)

The wild driver, the frustrated driver, the angry driver, the hurried and flustered driver, have all been indicted so frequently that we take it for granted that they are the villains. So they may be to some degree. But if they are it is not always directly. It is when they hand over to their deputy, the automatic pilot, that the mental state does the damage. Because of the emotions the deputy doesn't work so well, and the recall system is less reliable. An angry man, for example, fresh from a quarrel, hands over to his automatic pilot sometimes before he even gets into the car. He has no recollection of whether he shut the garage door, or how he got out on to the road. So we get the situation that a driver angered by a quarrel increases his vulnerabilities. A driver angered by other motorists is likely to pay more attention to the road, and not hand over to his automatic pilot at all. He could easily have fewer vulnerabilities than normal. This, I think, explains the wide variations in vulnerability rate recorded in Chapter 3 regarding angry drivers. The hurried driver may also be safe because he is concentrating on his driving.

Youth, as long as it is unsure of itself, has few accidents, even when driving atrociously. The accidents come with the cockiness of successful driving, and are often the first flights of an imperfect automatic pilot (always particularly lacking in visual perception). Many anxious drivers (a good many women for instance) obviously have no automatic pilot, and clock up astonishingly low accident rates, even though they seem so incompetent and unsafe.

All this is not just another way of saying that inattention is a major cause of accidents. It explains the mechanism of

inattention, at least in one aspect. It suggests, for example, that
the best of drivers, normally so safe, can once in a while slip
into atrocious inattention. This is not just carelessness. It is
because they are so accustomed to relying on their ultra-safe
deputy – the automatic pilot. There is, however, no way
(apart from the vulnerability technique) of their recognizing
when tiredness, anger, ill-health or preoccupations reach
the point where this deputy becomes – all at once out of
the blue – unreliable. The information that the automatic
pilot is below par reaches them suddenly, at a time
when they are ill-equipped to meet it, in the form of a
confrontation.

Quite clearly we can change this particular cause of accidents
quite dramatically if we can implant an awareness of vulnerabilities. These vulnerabilities will tend to attract conscious
attention just as easily whether it is the automatic pilot, or the
man himself, or his chauffeur, who is driving. We will then have
set up the same system of little nudges already referred to in
Chapter 7.

I have found the foregoing particularly helpful in winning
over the very able driver, who to begin with finds no attraction
in the vulnerability idea. He begins to see that even the best
do have sudden runs of vulnerabilities, which can have quite
an appreciable effect on their average.

10.3 Distractions. Passengers.
Mechanical Imperfections

There are many other causes of inattention besides mal-
functioning of the automatic pilot. Second in our list comes
inattention derived from distraction. It is not possible, for
instance, from an analysis of traffic accidents, to determine
whether passengers increase a driver's liability to accidents. No
normal driver has enough accidents for any statistical deductions to be drawn. By vulnerability rate measurements it is
extremely easy to establish it, and I have found, for example,
in my own case, that I make at least twice as many vulnerabilities as normal with certain passengers in the car. Some
distract me, some don't. It seems probable that this would be

a fairly general experience. It is something that the reader may readily determine for himself, once he has developed the vulnerability observation habit (and is, perhaps, quite a good example of how powerful this new technique is in showing us where we stand).

There is much evidence suggesting that minor mechanical difficulties, by their distracting effect, make a more important contribution to accidents than is generally realized. Even a slight difficulty in operating something such as a dipper switch can be enough to distract the driver at a crucial moment. The dipper switch is a particularly significant one, because, like badly aligned headlights, it causes a motorist coming in the opposite direction to flash his lights in protest and thus throw in a second distraction. It would be interesting to discover what proportion of dipper switches do give some minor trouble, at times. My guess would be at least 20% – by itself quite a substantial contribution to driver distraction.

Many other causes of distraction may be listed, such as coloured lights at night, sign postings that are hard to find or hard to read, dogs in the car, radio in the car, pretty girls in the car and on the sidewalk, and so on. The authorities work very steadily to reduce these wherever they can, and a wise driver will do the same.

10.4   Moods and Personalities

It is perhaps too much of a generalization to say that driver characteristics are responsible for accidents. Yet this is the factor which above all others defeats the professionals, the traffic planners and the police. Whatever they do, the personality of the driver tends to step in and defeat it. All serious workers are convinced that this is by far the largest single cause of accidents.

Much thought therefore has been devoted to the relationship between accidents and driver characteristics. Strong views are held that certain traits of personality, or certain moods, produce most of the accidents. There is much discussion as to what percentage of motorists are angry, naughty, wicked, criminal, uncivilized, frustrated, in a hurry, flustered, wishing to punish themselves, wishing to punish others, or upset by a row with their wives; and on what effect these moods have on accidents. Much elaborate and careful research work has been done on this. Traits of personality have been carefully investigated and correlated with accidents. A summary of the results, with references, is given in the Road Research Book (Bib. 1, Chapter 4), another in the preamble to the Spicer Report (Bib. 401).

These subdivisions are not yet very significant as a lead to action. All motorists at times qualify for one label or another. What causes the vulnerability is of secondary interest unless we can do something to stop it. As it is patently impossible to prevent these various attitudes and moods developing in a civilization, and as it is completely impracticable to label people as belonging to any one category, not much is gained by pursuing this line. The authorities continue to do all they can to ease things for the motorist, and avoid the unnecessary generation of bad moods, or inflaming of awkward personalities. They also try to discourage bad personalities by the machinery of the traffic law; and they mount propaganda drives against bad traits.

The basic need remains – for something which will operate to produce self restraint and discipline under stress. We have seen that to exhort or reason about this (9.1) or to appeal to the higher instincts (App. 8) or to try to teach it (9.2; App. 9), are all rather unpromising.

For our present purposes the most important aspect of personality factors is the mass of misapprehensions and inaccurate theories which cluster around them. Much misunderstanding centres around the following points in particular:

(a) *Wild Drivers*
We all know the wild driver who sails past, devoid of all courtesy and respect for the law, cutting in and out, passing on the wrong side, speeding and braking unnecessarily violently, and generally upsetting everyone on the road. We all assume that he is the cause of accidents, and we feel both angry and virtuous.

These odd cases of rabid driving that happen to come our way stir us so much that we tend to overestimate their number. They are of the order of one in a thousand (3.2b and App. 13).

One in a thousand is still quite a sizeable group, and it is worth considering how it is made up.

Some of these wild men belong to the high vulnerability group referred to in 3.2a. They are enormously dangerous, and very unaware of the risks they are forcing on others. Such are drunks, some types of wild youth, many criminals and a few ordinary drivers when in an abnormal state of mind. I suspect that the latter class is rare, and that the ordinary motorist in a bad state of mind may raise his vulnerability rate five or ten times, but scarcely a hundred. Also he probably seldom loses his awareness of major dangers. The data on police arrests indicate that probably four out of five in this group, the high vulnerability wild drivers, are drunks.

No individual stays in this group very long. He either reforms or is quickly eliminated by the police. Unfortunately, there are always new drunks and new wild youths, so that the group will always be with us. When we see a wild driver of this type we may at least comfort ourselves by the assurance that he won't last long. Either the police or an accident will get him, and we can afford to stay calm.

Another group of wild men are not nearly so dangerous. They may be termed the buccaneers – antisocial and wild but cunning. My observations are that there are a considerable number of these, with a vulnerability rate perhaps five or ten times normal. Others have a vulnerability rate much lower – even below average (see (c) below). The habitual buccaneer is too much on the look-out for the police to be easily eliminated. The occasional buccaneer, which is nearly all of us, is not misbehaving regularly enough to be eliminated either.

The buccaneer group of wild men is the one we may legitimately get angry about. They escape most of the accidents they deserve by virtue of the self-restraint of the rest. Only police omnipresence can eliminate them (11).

A third group of wild men are the unhandy drivers, who mean well but occasionally get themselves in a mess. Young drivers in particular are liable to do this. We should surely be patient with them.

I have followed a number of wild men and my observations suggest that this third group, the unhandy wild ones, is by far the largest and that we all join it at times. It is surprising to see how often after some miles the wild man appears to wake up to what he is doing and revert to normal behaviour. Who of us, for instance, has not at some time by accident cut in on another driver and thereafter tried to make it up to him by putting on more speed to make sure that he wasn't blocked again? Does our victim see it that way? Never! 'Damn speed hog!' he says.

The foregoing could well be ventilated in group discussion. This could do much to improve the general temper on the roads.

(b) *There are no Safe Drivers*

All drivers, even the safest, contribute to the 'cloud of threats' through which the motorist drives. Malfetti says (Bib. 402), 'driver behaviour at any moment is a point on a continuum, with safe driving at one end and unsafe driving at the other'. And later, 'most important is the understanding that for each driver, the unsafe end of the continuum can be reached. When sufficient negative forces are operative, no one is immune to unsafe driver behaviour.'

We have already seen (10.2) how the very safe driver can be trapped into relying on his automatic pilot, and (apart from observing vulnerabilities) has no means of knowing when this old friend is suddenly going to pack up on him.

(c) *Buccaneers, Racers, etc., and the Well-Behaved*

There is no evidence that the mature and socially co-operative driver is safer than the others. We all feel he must be, of course. But he may well not be. His ease of mind may well cause him to be more relaxed than the bad buccaneer, who drives selfishly but very much on the *qui vive*. The instinctive racer is usually very alert also, and very probably therefore safer than average.

My own observations on vulnerability rate rather indicate that when it comes to unusually safe driving a certain kind of skill, not personality, is the operative factor. Many of the outstandingly safe drivers that I have observed have the kind of personal characteristics which on current psychology would lead to the most unsafe driving. They are uncivilized, angry, antisocial, violate the law whenever they can, but do so with considerable cunning and are dead safe most of the time.

Like the other wild men they may well leave a trail of frustration and anger behind them that is a fruitful cause of accidents in others.

(d) *Tiredness*

Research has shown that tiredness is a big contributor towards accidents. This effect emerged in the vulnerability experiment. All the indications are that few aspects would be more worth working on than making drivers aware of the dangers of tiredness, particularly when combined with the dangers of driving in the dark (Bib. 3 and 309). This factor seems to be one that could particularly repay consideration in the discussion groups. It is the factor which is most likely to defeat attempts by the individual to reduce his risks (5.1).

Eysenck (Bib. 305 and 308, pp. 22, 30, 252) suggests that momentary rest pauses (in effect blackouts of attention) occur in the mind when tired or bored. This surely is significant enough to be seen as a separate and important cause of accident. It lends colour to the theory that the warnings from vulnerability observations should be heeded and driving abandoned before the situation has deteriorated too far. Clearly a vulnerability during a momentary blackout would not be observed.

(e) *Accident Repeaters*

Some people go on having accidents. Up to a point this is a matter of chance (see Chapter 2). There is some evidence, from insurance claims and police records, that those who have accidents are more likely than others to have more accidents (Bib. 1, p. 125 *et seq.*). It is a measure of the defeat which research has sustained so far in this field that there seems to be no accepted proposition for using this to reduce accidents.* No one can tell a man who is having accidents what he should do to stop having them. So numerous and so complex are the

* The account of some Canadian Clinics in Bib. 308 seems promising.

factors involved! Vulnerability observations are the answer to this. The man himself then makes his own diagnosis. He is the one man who can.

It might be thought that in view of the frightful slaughter involved we might be justified in barring a man from the roads, at least after he has had several accidents. Work done in Connecticut suggests that this would be ineffective, as we would expect from Chapter 2. An investigation of 20,000 drivers over two periods of three years showed that barring all those with two or more accidents in the first period would have eliminated only 4% of all accidents in the research period (Bib. 406). This is a very valuable yield, but the price in unfairness would be far too high, and the measure would not be tolerated by the general public.

The trouble about accident-repeaters is that, like wild men, they are not a homogeneous group. Some are victims of a run of bad luck. If one considers two accidents over a period of three years, it is almost certain that the greater proportion would be the result of random distribution. Such a group would be nearly all normal motorists with average vulnerability scores. At the other end of the spectrum are the wild men with a hundred times normal vulnerability, completely unaware of any danger. They may well have five or ten accidents a year. In between are the unhandy drivers, new-comers or congenitally unskilled, with perhaps ten times the normal vulnerability rate. Others are habitually second-rate drivers; others are the occasional outrageous drivers.

The type of accident produced by the hundred-fold men is often more violent than normal, frequently with fatalities (3.2a). Such a driver, if he makes a habit of it, is mostly picked up quickly by the police, not only by repetition of violations, but also often by one very bad violation involving disqualification of licence. Some of these hundred-fold drivers, however, are clearly extremely cunning in keeping a look-out for the police, and it is these that become one part of the accident-repeater group. While they manage to avoid citations they are statistically indistinguishable from the less dangerous types, except perhaps by the violence of their accidents.

Clearly accident-repeaters are not a group which can be

investigated as a guide to the cause of accidents. They are far too abnormal and far too heterogeneous for any deduction made from them as a group to apply to normal motorists.

It would pay handsomely to make a special drive on people who have had repeated accidents, to try to persuade them to count their vulnerabilities from now on. This, properly handled, would really work (App. 12).

(f) *Effect of Specific Personal Qualities*

If we come to think of any one specific personal quality, whether of physique such as eyesight or of character such as quarrelsomeness, we find that there is little evidence available that any one of these characteristics, or their absence, causes accidents. They may well do so (to a very limited degree – see 2.5), but in the statistics their effect is masked by the many other factors involved. For example, extensive and accurate tests show no direct relationship between even extreme aggressive tendencies and liability to repeated accidents (Bib. 401). People with bad peripheral vision, or who find difficulty in taking quick decisions, or who react very slowly, would all, one would have expected, tend to have more accidents than the average. Yet the odds are so little affected that no one has been able to establish that this is so.

We have also seen that in any accident two people and their characteristics are nearly always involved, so that the isolation of any one characteristic and its effect is clearly impossible. For example, the driver who is very wild and careless may well experience more confrontations than the average. But he may be exceptionally skilled in handling his car, and thus successfully negotiate many more close shaves than the average driver. Or, a driver may have poor vision or slow reactions (perhaps due to alcohol) and as a result may tend to crash every time he meets a situation demanding these qualities. But he may be so careful and so defensive in his driving that he escapes the confrontations where his defects are dangerous.

An exception to this in the case of visual perception has already been studied in the early chapters.

(g) *Summary*

The foregoing examples of driver mood and personality are

sufficient to show that we cannot easily identify the dangerous driver. We can indeed identify certain groups or kinds of motorists by behaviour patterns. But the individuals constituting the group are not the same from day to day. Moods are more significant than personalities. Most of us at times join the ranks of the wild men or the buccaneers or, if not the drunk, at least the drinkers. Many of us drive once in a while like accident repeaters. Many of us on occasion become as unhandy as the veriest tyro. Attempts to label individuals, whether by psychological tests, by descriptions of personality or by statistical deductions, will not help much to reduce accidents. We must address ourselves to all drivers.

10.5 Other Factors

(a) *The Pedestrian*

The analysis of the collision given in Chapter 2 appears to apply, unchanged, when one of the parties is a pedestrian. One group of qualities involving visual perception and caution determine whether a pedestrian becomes vulnerable. A second group help determine whether he successfully dodges a confrontation.

The main difference from the motorist is that the pedestrian is not emotionally involved with his walking as the average driver is with his driving. There is not the need to break down any closed mind or induce any new restraints in the pedestrian. Inattention, distraction and unawareness are the main factors, especially in children and in the aged.

The best way to protect pedestrians is by segregation, e.g. off-the-road shopping centres, subways and bridges, traffic lights and special crossing places. This and the training of young children represents a major part of the activity of the authorities. A comprehensive analysis of the U.K. approach to this is given in the Road Safety Book (Bib. 1, Chapters 3 and 7).

It would seem that a considerable proportion of the accidents to older pedestrians are due to momentary absent-mindedness while crossing roads. The habit of scanning instead of trying to reason as one looks would reduce this and might make quite a sensational improvement. By scanning is meant the idea of letting one's eyes travel over the whole field around one all the time while preparing to cross and crossing. Pilots in the war were taught to keep their head and eyes moving over the whole field in this way, on the basis that an attacker could come from any side. This is so nearly the case in crossing a road that it is surely a good principle.

There is also quite some doubt as to whether the instruction to children 'Look right, look left, look right again' (or *vice versa*) is really the soundest advice. It does not always cater for traffic coming from behind them, from a side road. There seems little doubt that it is positively bad advice for anyone who travels from right rule to left rule countries. The advice to scan would surely be not much more difficult to teach to children and would be applicable to all pedestrians in all countries.

(b) *Mechanical Failures*

Estimates of the part played by mechanical failures range from 4% to about 30%. The current 'hunch' – it can be little more – seems to be about 10%, but recent work by Moseley (Bib. 306) suggests it might be much more important than this. A very small failure may be sufficient to distract and trigger off a major accident(10.2).

Some astonishing results attended a drive in England in 1964 on the mechanical condition of heavy commercial vehicles. It was disclosed that an incredibly unsafe condition was common. Often this derived from the pressures of commercial competition, or from drivers prepared to accept any imperfections rather than risk losing their jobs.

The situation differs widely in different communities. In some cities there is a tradition of careful service. In others a car returns from every visit to a service depot with two or three new faults. There is an ethical problem here which is discussed in 11.1.

As an example of the uncertainty in this sphere the U.K. Road Safety Book (Bib. 1, p. 429) suggests that the effect of inadequate rear lights might well be five times as operative as appears from official figures. This book makes out a strong case for regular mechanical inspection as an answer to this.

There is a widespread hunch that regular mechanical inspection is not enough. An inspection is needed every time a car returns from a repair shop. I have seen so many cases of shocking carelessness by mechanics that I am prejudiced in this matter, and could well believe that the basic cause of at least 25% of accidents is mechanical trouble. I get the strong impression that this percentage rises each year. The blame for this lies chiefly with greedy commercial exploiters of the repair business plus the plans made by car manufacturers to give service via their agents at foolishly low prices. Everyone in the trade will recognize what I am talking about.

Whether the figure is 10% or 25%, it is clearly important enough to justify detailed study. What can be done about it? Certainly no half measures can succeed. The carelessness must be located and sheeted home. This implies the establishment of inspection centres which can be used by any motorist on his way home from a repair shop. He should be able to call in and not only get the repair checked but get an overall search made for any new faults that have been created. Until this is done he should regard his car as a potential death trap. Where a fault is located this should then be tracked back to the mechanic concerned and a major issue made of it.

Who should pay? Obviously the motorist must. If he is wise he will be glad to.

Who could take the initiative in establishing such centres? Clearly the insurance companies and the motorists' associations.

In England the M.A.A. have established a Fidelity Scheme for repair shops which shows that the motor agents are aware of this problem.

The establishment of such centres is not a big undertaking. Premises and a good manager are all that are needed. There is no occasion to start it on anything more than a very small scale. It would probably be some time before demand for the service built up. When that happened the expansion would be self-stimulating.

Such a scheme is only a slight – but very important – change in direction from services already offered by many associations. It is the wielding a big stick over the repair shops and the individual mechanics concerned that the associations are reluctant to tackle. Yet this is the prime objective, and must be accepted.

(c) *Wrong Sense of Values*

An important factor is an inadequate philosophy – a failure to think out the relative values in a situation. A motorist will risk a crash merely to satisfy some small facet of personal pride – showing some other completely unknown motorist that he won't be put upon, etc. Such a man has never worked out relative values. How important is it really that this unknown motorist should be scored off? What would he be prepared to pay in money for the satisfaction? I doubt if you could persuade him to put his hand on his pocket-book. Yet he will risk an accident that could blind him for life. For what figure would he sell his eyes? A million pounds? Five million dollars?

A suggestion with regard to this has been made in 9.11, on teaching young people a certain attitude.

10.6 What Makes Motorists Take Risks?

Here is a list of the main reasons why motorists take risks:

(a) Anger, which inhibits the operation of fear and of the social instinct.

(b) A period of frustration (the most patient generally behave most badly when their patience finally snaps).

(c) Extraneous emotional upsets (e.g. quarrel with wife or boss).

(d) Worry, or a preoccupation with some trouble.

(e) To catch up on time.

(f) The boredom of a long drive (see Bib. 307 – suggesting that 90% accidents on M.1 are due to falling asleep.)

(g) Tiredness.

(h) The instincts of youth – rivalry, racing, showing-off.

(i) Pride in or other emotional involvement in car.

(j) Instinctive arrogance and selfishness; barbarian instincts generally.

(k) Inattention and distraction.

(l) Wrong sense of values.

It will be seen that there is little hope of eliminating any of these factors from our world by present methods, except as described in Chapter 9 (by establishing a new social habit in the minds of the young and waiting for the present generation to die off). There is no motivation available to us strong enough for propaganda to triumph over these feelings in the mind of the average motorist (see App. 8).

Counting vulnerabilities can do it however – see Chapter 7.

10.7 Reducing the Damage. Seat Belts

A great deal is known about the effect of high deceleration on the body, from aircraft and rocket research, and from research by manufacturers and laboratories in the motor-car field. Very little use seems to be made of what is known. The basic reason for this seems to be a dislike by the manufacturers to do anything to remind the customers of such an unpleasant aspect of the product. One can see what an effect it could have on sales, particularly on the preposterous fairy tale images which we have been considering in earlier chapters. The high proportion of car advertisements that contain pictures of lovely girls and a background suggesting glamorous social functions, indicates how important a role this kind of image plays in car salesmanship.

In order to get a mental picture of the damage involved, one can picture the whole dashboard, windscreen, steering-wheel, etc., turned 90 deg., so that it looks upward instead of backward. The driver and passenger can then picture themselves held in the air at different heights, corresponding to different speeds, and allowed to drop under the action of gravity on to this set-up. This is described in more detail in Appendix 4. The average motorist has almost no conception whatever of the forces involved, and strangely enough no one makes any propaganda to inform him. Anyone who has walked into the edge of a door at 3 m.p.h. can testify to the astonishing bruises that can be achieved even at such a low speed. It is quite easy to kill by a 15 m.p.h. impact. It is almost impossible not to kill by a 30 m.p.h. impact.* Most impacts in practice take place at lower effective speeds than is generally realized because of last moment brakings, cushioning or 'give' in parts of the structure, and indirectness of impact.

This raises a doubt as to the wisdom of claiming too much for seat belts. It is often said that they make speeds up to 50 m.p.h. quite safe. Yet their greatest value is probably for city speeds. As it is, motorists with no conception of a 30 m.p.h. crash feel they don't need to put them on for city driving.

Many people claim that seat belts cause motorists to step-up their driving to the point where they are in greater danger than they were without them. Certainly Smeed's 15% estimated reduction (10.1 and Bib. 3) is not yet proven.

The major technical problem in reducing damage from impacts is how to dispose of the kinetic energy. Rubber cushions or elastic seat belts are of little use for this reason, and can actually increase the amount of damage by increasing the maximum deceleration (Bib. 1 p. 481). This is best expressed in lay language by saying that any elastic device causes a rebound, so that the motorist's body is not just stopped, but is thrown backwards. What is actually needed is not something elastic, but something which gives way in stages, absorbing energy with each breakage. Various cellular structures can be obtained to do this. The horror with which the average motorist views them is a measure of his utter unawareness of how serious an impact can be. 'What?' he exclaims, 'do you suggest I hit my head against that lump of hard stuff and that will reduce the damage.' Poor chap! We must try to persuade him to walk into a few more doors.

Simple belts, which allow the top part of the body to fly forward are generally thought to be less safe than harnesses, which hold the shoulders back. I suppose this depends on what the body is going to hit when it flies forward. It you hold the shoulders back, with some people the chin hits the chest

*Would you be prepared to run into a brick wall at 30 m.p.h.? Would you if it had a 12-inch layer of foam rubber on it? With the rubber the minimum deceleration, neglecting bounce, would be over 30g. In practice it would be nearer 50g., i.e. a force applied to your body of 50 times its weight – say three or four tons. You can picture a crane placing a four-ton gravestone gently on top of you for a moment. However brief the moment, you would crack like a nut.

before the neck breaks; with others, the neck snaps off first.

This is a painful subject. There are, nevertheless, a few leads that are worth recording, because they do offer a useful field of activity for anyone who wishes to do something to help:

(a) *Energy-Absorbing Seat Belts*

It should be quite possible to develop a seat harness, as distinct from a belt, which allows the body to travel forward through some energy-absorbing material* (such as a block of cellular plastic to which the harness is anchored and through which the anchor is arranged to plough). At low speeds of impact this would give the neck a chance to decelerate the head without breaking it off. A series of short films, or demonstrations along the lines of the dropping techniques described in Appendix 4 might then persuade people to put these harnesses on when they are driving around town. A very substantial reduction in the number of serious accidents in the cities could result.

The exercise here is a major one – to get a completely new picture into the mind of the average motorist. It is as big an assignment as that proposed in Chapter 6 for getting across the vulnerability idea.

(b) *Seat Conformation*

At odd periods in history there have been chairs designed to rest the back of the head. Aeroplane seats sometimes do this. Surely it should not be too difficult to include such a seat in the modern car, and still not destroy the fairy tale image? It could be tied to comfort, instead of safety. It would completely eliminate one type of major injury – that now termed 'whiplash'. This comes from the punch in the back which sends the body flying forward when a car is hit from behind, and flicks the head back.

It is rare to find a complete answer available in this way, and a pity that it has not yet been made use of.† The trouble with all

---

*A Dutch manufacturer has developed special shock-absorbent stitching which has been approved by the RAI-TNO Research Institute for Road Vehicles. Delft. (116/136).

†It is understood that Messrs. Cox of Watford, England, are developing such a seat.

precautions of this kind is that no one believes that it's going to happen to him, and can't bring himself to go out of his way at all to cater for it. Such a step therefore could only be a sales risk.

(c) *Conformation of Dash*

Some attempts have been made to equip dashboards with an energy-absorbing layer. Combined with an easy-shatter windscreen this could be of great value.

Almost certainly a magic improvement could be made by treating the front seat complete with harness as a capsule and arranging for energy-absorbing material to be interpolated between the capsule and the front of the car. There are several feet of travel available by this means which should absorb a 30 m.p.h. impact (about 11g. for 3 ft.) without damaging anybody. It would not be an easy mechanical problem – the windscreen and dash would have to start moving forward ahead of the human bodies. But it is not an insoluble mechanical problem. One wonders whether some of the big manufacturers could not be persuaded to sink £40,000 or £50,000 or $100,000 into developing something of this kind. As an extra, costing perhaps 30% of the total value of the car, it might even have a commercial application. Anyone who has seen a few fruity accidents might gladly pay that much to get it.

An alternative would be to build out the front of the car by a foot or two of energy-absorbing material. This might well be cheap and could possibly be done with actual improvement to appearance.

(d) *First Aid*

We have said that one can, on the average, count on 20 to 30 years or more safe driving without a crash. This means that roughly one in twenty or thirty cars will have a crash this year. How many drivers have catered for the crash by carrying a first aid kit? I would say not one in fifty. How many, if they saw their wife with a great hole in her belly and blood gushing out, would know what to do? Probably about the same proportion! Not so long ago I met a policeman who seemed a little dazed.

He had discovered a heap of crashed cars in the middle of Sydney Harbour bridge, with no human being around at all – a sort of *Marie Celeste*. He got off his bike and wandered around to see what he could find. After a bit he discovered a human forearm lying on the ground. (This accident, due to driving with an elbow resting on the open window, is more common than is realized.) The motorists concerned had flagged a passing car, and rushed off to hospital. Imagine the difference that a little first-aid knowledge and a first-aid kit could make in a case like this. Imagine that ride to the hospital, probably with nothing whatever available.

This is all an unhappy part of our subject. Better reduce our vulnerabilities, and not have the accidents.

CHAPTER 11

The Police and the Law

11.1 Ethics

ONE cannot get very far with the problems of law and its enforcement without first considering the ethical principles on which it is based. Let us take a look at four typical problems.

(*a*) If carelessness in tightening one nut in an aeroplane results in 150 people being killed, how serious is that carelessness? If a mechanic neglects a brake rod which thereafter piles up eight people in a death pyre, is this a crime? or a sin? Is the careless mechanic to be arraigned on earth? or in heaven? Nevil Shute chose this particular case as the basis of his 'Round the Bend', and suggested (though not in these words) that the price list of sins has to be rewritten every thousand years or so.

(*b*) Is cutting a corner a mild or a serious offence, when it causes two other cars full of people to be completely wrecked? I knew a case where this actually happened, and the culprit was out of sight and not even involved.

(*c*) Should a mother who tucks up her child in an inflammable nightgown and leaves an open radiator in the bedroom be punished? And should this happen only when the child has been burned to death?

(*d*) A young girl is worried about the strange behaviour of a man who could well be a maniac. She goes to the police for protection. Is it right that they should say to her (in effect) 'Sorry! we'll give you protection after he's proved he's a maniac by attacking you'.

The practical answers to *c* and *d* are quite clear. We don't punish unwitting negligence, or simple stupidity. We don't treat a man as dangerous until we know he is. The price of this in burnt children and raped innocents is a bit high, but much thought and much legal experiment has found it to be the best compromise. Cases *a* and *b* are fairly close to *c* and *d*, respectively, in general framework. In these also, if we follow established practice we cannot make too much of one small carelessness in the workshop or one minor piece of bad driving on the roads. So many of these are perpetrated without doing any harm.

Yet the ethics of these situations do not support this at all. The stupid mother is culpable. There is a moral obligation to protect the child and the defenceless girl. We sacrifice them only as a practical measure. Must we do the same for the road casualties? There are so many more of them!

What practical guidance does the law give on this? None! The unions, meanwhile, frame up in pugilistic stance at any suggestion of tightening up on carelessness in the shop. The general public brings a schoolboy outlook to the party, drives selfishly and breaks the law whenever it thinks it can get away with it.

It is impossible to give this matter careful thought without reaching the conviction that the careless mechanic and the dangerous driver are committing greater ethical errors than are yet reflected in the law. Over a period of time, as these problems are slowly digested, we shall certainly see a hardening of the law against these sinners.* This problem is explored further in Appendix 7.

In considering any practical aspect of law administration, such as the police, we are clearly entitled therefore to give preference to this trend. When in doubt we should err on the side of being as severe as possible on offences that lead to road accidents.

There are many such ethics/law problems requiring consideration. They are basically a professional matter. One such – making discourtesy an offence – is adumbrated in Appendix 17. (See also Bib. 612).

11.2 The Probability Picture

Many misunderstandings about traffic problems derive from

---

* Since the above was written an airline has sued a manufacturer for the cost of a major crash because it was due to a loose screw on one instrument from this manufacturer.

an unawareness of the length of the odds, or a failure to appreciate the magnitudes involved. Deductions which would be correct in ordinary life simply don't apply in this region. Let us take the familiar example from roulette. The odds in favour of black and red are identical. If the ball is rolled often enough the number of times red comes up is very closely equalled by black. The more times the ball is rolled the closer the percentage of reds and blacks approaches 50/50. There is a mathematical law relating the probability of a given deviation from the 50% to the number of throws. But this law cannot predict what will happen on any one individual throw. There may be five reds or five blacks in a row.

Apply this to the traffic case. Suppose you and I are equally good or equally bad drivers, and deserve the same punishment at law. If we are caught let us say 100 times then we are likely to show somewhere around 50 convictions each. But, if we are only apprehended on the average once in four years, which is roughly the average achieved in practice (once in seven years in England, once in 2½ years in California*) then it is quite possible for me to be punished five times in a ten-year period and for you not at all. If this actually happens it is extremely hard to convince the authorities that it is a run of luck and that in point of fact I am no worse a driver than you are.

Even people who will accept the above proposition when there is no difference between you and me find it very hard to see if there is a known difference between us. If I am, to their knowledge, a much worse driver than you, say four times as bad, it is almost impossible to convince them that you might well be apprehended more frequently than me. With real distress they say to me 'but the odds are four to one! So you *must* be caught more often.' Yet this is completely untrue when the total number of apprehensions is small. With an average of one apprehension in four years, and allowing for some difference in cunning between us, it might take fifty years before the true situation began to emerge in the statistics, and perhaps two hundred years before it could be regarded as proven.

With the present numbers of police actually operating on the roads (in any country) it would certainly take far too long

* On the basis of one car one driver. The true figure could well be 50% worse.

for any distinction to become evident, with only a four to one difference. (Also individual driving habits do not remain constant over such a long period.) Only the outrageously bad ones, with perhaps a hundred times the average violation rate, are shown up quickly by the frequency of the arrests. Even some of these very bad cases, as we saw in connection with accident-repeaters (10.4e) develop such skill in keeping a look-out for the police, that they do not readily show up in the arrests. ("arrests" = "citations").

Fortunately, cunning in avoiding the police is rarely completely effective. It only increases the time required to get to the multiple score. Thus certain youths and some criminals, who appear to belong to the hundredfold vulnerability group, are shown up by multiple citations in the long run (Bib. 302).

It will now be clear why in practice there is no noticeable correlation between citations and accidents until the score gets fairly high. A man with two or three citations over a year does not have more accidents than average; nor does a man with two or three accidents appear more frequently than usual in the citations. To anyone without understanding of the probabilities this would appear to show firstly, that violations of traffic law don't produce accidents, and secondly, that the traffic laws don't help in preventing accidents. Common sense, and everyone's hunch, says that this is wrong. Of course it is, and the probabilities explain why it sometimes may not appear that way. A correlation begins to emerge, as one would expect, when accidents or citations reach four or five and the individual becomes very clearly highlighted when the scores get higher than this.

This is an excellent example of the difficulty of proof in this field, the complexities of trying to make any simple deduction, and the need to think in terms of probabilities.

It is amusing to see the reaction of indignation which seems to boil up when the average motorist discovers that his bookings are largely matters of chance. He appears to remember some occasion when he was booked, and feels aggrieved. The logical reaction should be 'So that's why I got away with all those cases of bad driving without punishment!'

A similar elusive probability picture exists with regard to

violations of the law. ('Violation' should not be confused with 'citation', 'arrest', 'summons', 'booking' or 'ticket', which we have been considering above.) A motorist commits many 'violations' or 'infringements' before he is actually caught. Estimates vary widely as to how many. The figure frequently used is 600 average. The lowest estimate I met from any police force was 50 average. Much depends on how a continuing violation is counted. One method is to regard a stretch of road visible to one observer (such as a police patrol) as the unit. A motorist continuing to exceed the speed limit is regarded as making a separate violation for each stretch of road. On this basis of counting, the number of violations per day made by the average motorist varies enormously in different areas. In many places a blind eye has to be turned to violations of speed limit during peak periods, because otherwise the traffic would jam up. The number of violations per driver must then run into hundreds a day, and there is probably less than one violation booked in a hundred thousand. In more fortunate places where the speed limit is enforceable it seems probable that some motorists rarely break the law at all.

These matters lend themselves to simple traffic calculations. For example, when we know the number of patrols and the number of bookings we can estimate the order of magnitude of the violations committed by the average motorist. This has been done in Appendix 13, using figures which are fairly close to the English situation. The answer works out to about 50 per annum, which strangely enough lines up quite closely with the American estimates of one violation booked in 300-600. (English bookings average once in seven years, i.e. 350 violations for one booked.) Yet we know in fact that the violations per motorist in England run into thousands per annum, chiefly due to a widespread disregard of speed limits. Two explanations come to mind: either the police turn a blind eye (as indeed they have to), or motorists keep a watch for the police, and moderate speed and behaviour when they know they are under observation. (As indeed they do. In fact, wherever one finds a stream of traffic scrupulously adhering to the speed limits, one can deduce with near certainty that there is a police car ahead.)

We have seen that vulnerabilities produce accidents. We have seen that violations produce citations. We have seen that a motorist's vulnerability rate largely determines the number of his accidents, and that there is a fairly constant figure (50,000 to 100,000) relating vulnerabilities to accidents. We have seen that there is no such relation between his violations and his citations, because so much depends upon his skill in keeping a lookout for the police, and also upon police practices in sometimes turning a blind eye to certain classes of violations.* What needs to be added is that if the police were able to enforce the law uniformly, and if the police were able to establish a sense of omnipresence (11.5) this situation would change and there would be a specific relation between a motorist's violations and his citations. This is the ideal, and we consider in the following sections how it can be approached.

To round off the picture we should repeat that there is no constant relationship to be expected between violations and vulnerabilities of any motorist, normal or otherwise. We have seen how one man may be relatively unaware of dangers but meticulous or cunning regarding rules. He might score few violations but high vulnerabilities. Another might be normal for most of the time, but suffer from a change of mood and change his score pattern. The possible variations are endless, and not apparently worth attempting to analyse or classify.

11.3   Public Irresponsibility

The situation described in the previous section makes it difficult for the general public to see breaches of road law in the same light as other breaches of the law. If you went out burgling 600 times before you were caught and saw everyone else doing the same, you would find it hard to take the crime of burglary very seriously. Certainly not if, when you were caught, the penalty were a small fine. In reality the *results* of traffic accidents

---

* This suggests that a motorist, like a girl's figure, can be described by three vital numbers. These are his vulnerabilities, his violations and his citations. From these we might deduce the number of accidents, and the number of very violent accidents which he can expect. This sounds good, but is completely unprofitable because of the considerations advanced in 10.4 regarding moods and shift in personality.

indicate that the crime of bad driving is much worse than that of burglary. Yet everyone sees it as much less. In the face of all the slaughter and distress, motoring is still some kind of 'teacher versus schoolboy' game. The police are expected to 'play fair' and 'be sporting'. The motorist is expected to adhere to schoolboy loyalties and a schoolboy type of behaviour in which it is clever to buck authority. The law is seen as a set of rather foolish rules for ninnies, which the manly man side-steps cunningly wherever possible. No disgrace attaches to doing this. Being caught calls for sympathy, because it can happen to anyone.

This attitude was well established years ago when the law really was outrageously foolish and motorists had to band together and put scouts on the roads to help protect themselves from persecution by the police. It was reinforced in the days – not yet quite left behind – when the motorist was seen as a legitimate means of replenishing local funds. The probability picture ensures that it will stay with us. As long as being booked for a traffic offence is purely a matter of chance – which it clearly is in *nearly* all cases – the public will sense this, unless we can handle the matter with a good deal of subtlety (11.4).

This situation would not be perhaps quite so bad but for the word 'nearly' in the foregoing sentence, because amongst all the minor violations there are some really flagrant breaches of the law that need to be punished severely and at once. The general condonation gives these bad cases much protection, so that we find, for example, the punishment for killing two people on the roads in one case only a fine of £25.

I wonder if it is generally realized just how difficult this is for the police. Here is an example. I was telling a friend about an announcement by the Chief of Police of New York, who said in effect (1964) that he would not recognize any obligation to be a 'sportsman' in trying to stop people killing others on the roads. My friend was a member of the local road safety council, experienced and mature. Yet I discovered he was almost shaking with fury over this. 'I suppose he would put disguised police cars on the roads, hide behind hedges, and that kind of unforgiveable trick,' he said. As, to my way of thinking, nothing could be more reasonable, I let it drop. But the strength of the prejudice is typical and most disturbing.

All this makes the technique of enforcing traffic laws basically different from other kinds of police activity. With other kinds of crime the police can go ahead on well established lines, catch the criminal, and be reasonably sure of public approval and even appreciation. Not so with traffic cases. As with traffic education, completely different techniques are needed. The criminal in this case is the general public – in England about 14 million of him, and in the U.S.A. no less than 55% of the entire population.

Even though many of the crimes committed on the roads are more serious than the orthodox crimes such as burglary, much could be said for treating them on a different basis and using perhaps a different terminology for all except the more serious. It is possible that even the use of the word 'criminal' (compare Bib. 302) can antagonize the general public, and that a different and milder word could be adopted. Richardson (Bib. 612) emphasizes a need to discriminate between civil offences and criminal offences on the roads. If everyone is a criminal, then no one is a criminal.

Another encouragement to public irresponsibility derives from insurance practices. A. M. Glen thinks that the absence of any financial stake by the driver plays a considerable part in this. The bill for an accident is always met by the insurance company or by the driver's employer – hardly ever by the driver. This is confirmed by Alan Brehaut, who cites a case where an accident-repeater with six or seven claims in a little over a year disappeared from the records entirely when his policy was rewritten so that he bore the first £100 costs.

British insurance companies say that they regularly apply such methods, often quite early in the career of a claim repeater. But they do not appear to publicize this, possibly for fear of losing business.

This factor could be of very great significance. Alan Brehaut thinks that a complete statutory bar on anyone except the driver paying the first £50 (surely a very mild measure) would make a sensational reduction (perhaps 33 to 50%) in both accidents and insurance premiums.

Such a statutory measure might at first sight appear likely to reduce only the scratch and dent type of accident. But this would not be so at all, because the increased care and awareness induced would result in a reduction of vulnerabilities generally, and thus reduce all types of accidents, including the most violent, in about the same proportion.

Quite a simple piece of research by an insurance company would be sufficient to check the above hunches and give guidance to legislators. It is hoped that someone will speedily tackle this, as the figure of 33 to 50% reduction is the largest claimed for any sober proposal.

11.4 Getting Tough. Demerit Marks

We have seen that the basic ethical trend should be to get tough (11.1); that it is a crying need for the good of youth (9.2); that it is the only immediate solution to the hard core problem (6.1). Getting tough is also clearly one way of breaking the general public's irresponsible approach described in the previous section.

This does not imply that the police should bully or frighten. What is clearly needed is some form of intimidation which does not antagonize. It must not induce a sense of anxiety such as might affect driving skill. The phrase 'intimidation without antagonizing' could well be the watchword.

They must, unfortunately, intimidate. Nothing which does not penetrate to the level of the basic emotions will restrain the angry, the hurried, the uncivilized, and the closed mind. (See for example Bib. 603.) Nothing else will curtail the folly of barbarian youth. Nothing else will jolt the fatuous ass of a grown-up schoolboy out of his irresponsibility.

The police obviously cannot afford to antagonize the general public – which is no easy problem when anything in the way of getting tough is bound to be outrageously unfair. This must be the case when the selection of people to punish, as described in 11.2, is little more than a random selection. There is no harm in picking people to be punished on a random basis, when all deserve punishment. Everyone commits traffic crimes. We only catch a small proportion of them and these are the ones we punish. The fact that others escape is irrelevant. But if we want to make an example of those we catch, and punish them more severely than the crime really warrants, it becomes much more difficult to avoid active communal resentment.

The problem is further complicated by the presence of a proportion of motorists of goodwill, who will respond to gentle treatment better than to the tough approach (e.g. Bib 11). It is imperative not to push them off-side.

Thus getting tough by making examples of people, with a heavy penalty, is not a practical proposition at all. It is too much like shooting every tenth soldier to encourage the other nine.

There are other ways of intimidation besides severe punishment. For instance, an impressive court hearing can be most effective, even if the punishment at the end is quite light. Unfortunately, this costs too much. Already the cases that must come to court are overloading the legal machinery (in all countries) and forcing the police in the direction of tickets and on-the-spot judgements. Imagine staging a million fully panoplied court cases a year in England alone. (In 1963 there were 1,054,232 prosecutions.)

A better proposition is to intimidate by the threat of severe punishment, without immediately applying it.* If a motorist picked up and punished mildly for a mild crime realizes that this starts a process which can end with a severe penalty such as the loss of his licence, he will start to be careful right away, without necessarily being antagonized. Systems which keep a record of past violations and perhaps accidents provide a mounting effect of this kind which can be most effective, and which stays always present in the motorist's mind. These are conveniently termed demerit marking systems or cumulative penal systems.

Antagonism to cumulative systems due to apparent unfairness can be diminished by increasing the number of tickets or bookings which bring down the penalties. This means increasing the number of patrols. If a man gets two tickets for minor offences in a year and is then penalized, while the average is one per year, his two are obviously pure chance and one cannot

* A. E. O'dell puts it thus – a punishment loses its power when it is inflicted.

punish him very heavily without antagonizing. But if this heavy punishment descends only after four of five apprehensions and warnings it is clearly much more probable that the penalty is deserved. Also, he will in his heart accept the blame – which is the operative factor in avoiding antagonism. (The psychologist says he acquires a feeling of guilt – an essential factor in the structure of society.)

The same result can be achieved in any other way which makes the culprit *think* he is being treated fairly. Justice doesn't come into it.

The best compromise clearly is to choose a heavy penalty (itself a problem, see 11.9) combined with a system of cumulative or demerit marks extending over long enough periods for there to be a reasonable appearance of justice. A validity period of two years, with say, five valid marks calling down the penalty could surely produce little antagonism. Given a slight warning at three, a strong one at four, the fives will become very rare. From the actual statistics as to the number of motorists receiving two, three, four or more tickets, such a scheme can be designed to produce whatever degree of pressure the local mood will take. Adjustments each year can be made in accordance with this mood, by varying the pressures at three, four and five. (See also Bib. 612. Napley.)

At first sight this may seem a callous and cynical approach. It is, however, the nearest approach to fair treatment that can be given with the facilities available.

Demerit marks systems are now being used in many places. It is not always realized that it is now (since 1962) incorporated into the English system on the basis of three marks over three years producing a six month suspension of licence. In my discussions it was surprising how many motorists – particularly taxi-drivers and other professionals – advocated the idea in one form or another.

It is surprising how quickly a community will respond to a tough approach. I observed such an attempt in detail in one community a few years ago. This was organized with considerable skill and with correct and helpful behaviour from the patrols. After a few months one began to notice odd motorists who had clearly decided that they would conform to the rules.

They would be adhering to 30 m.p.h. while the rest sailed happily by at 45–50. Suddenly – as if a wand had been waved – the pattern changed and the majority conformed. Driving on the route I followed had been a daily nightmare. It became a pleasure, with all sense of danger gone. I've never known such a sensational change in public behaviour, apart from wartime. Unfortunately in this case too much antagonism developed and the police had to retreat. It took about six months for the traffic to revert to the old bad behaviour.

The cost of increasing patrols is not quite as fearsome as might be expected. In most areas the force actually on the roads is quite a small proportion of the total police force and could well be doubled without a disastrous cost increase. A ticket system in place of court prosecution enables an immediate increase by cutting down court attendances by the patrols.

11.5   Omnipresence. Mechanical Devices

In the previous section we said that to get tough without antagonizing we must aim to be fair. This can only be achieved by increasing patrols. Increased patrols are effective in other ways. In fact in safety circles it is generally accepted that increasing patrols is the most effective way of all of reducing traffic accidents. Smeed's figure of 25% reduction by this means (10.1) is not a round figure but is calculated from experimental results which he quotes. Not everyone will concede that this improvement is due to intimidation. But this seems to be chiefly a dislike of the connotations of the word. One man who indignantly repudiated 'intimidation', was quite content with 'discouragement', which surely means the same thing in this context.

Once the need for intimidation is accepted a very significant point emerges, namely, that the possibility of the police being present can be as effective as their actual presence. The double conception 'the police must not be bucked, the police are everywhere' is surely the perfect deterrent.* It will induce restraint

---

* Those with a misconception of the nature of liberty may tend to mutter 'Big Brother is watching you'. Yet the only liberty being restricted is the freedom to misbehave!

in most minds however closed, however angry, tired, etc. This suggests a second watchword for police techniques 'intimidation plus omnipresence'.

Many ways of achieving this have been suggested. I never cease to be astonished at the motorists' reactions to them. One man accepts an idea that gives another man a fit. Here are some:

(a) *Plain Clothes Patrols*

It is suggested that a proportion of patrols – both on foot and in cars – should not be recognizable as police.

The proportion need not be high. It is only necessary that the public should know they exist, and should occasionally come in contact with evidence of their activities.

Unrecognizable patrols are clearly much less effective than uniformed ones as regards direct discouragement. They only impinge directly on those they book, whereas the recognizable patrol disciplines the traffic automatically just by being seen. On the other hand, the cunning violator is warned when he recognizes a police patrol and reverts to bad behaviour only when they are out of sight. The unrecognizable patrols deter him and also sometimes catch him. Their effect in reducing the thousands of unbooked violations referred to in 11.2 can be sensational.

An objection frequently raised to plain clothes patrols is that they may be mistaken for gangsters. This apparently is a more serious matter than would be appreciated by the ordinary public. Perhaps some "Police" sign, not easily duplicated, could be displayed mechanically when required.

(b) *Speed Traps*

A useful effect is achieved by notices on a particular stretch of road telling motorists that speed traps sometimes operate there (e.g. by radar devices). There is no obligation to operate them all the time, nor to say when they are being operated.

No motorist who observes the law should mind this. But very many do. This reflects the basic difficulty over speed limits, which is discussed in Section 11.7.

(c) *Photographic Devices and Speed Indicators*

It is now a very simple matter to read a passing motorist's speed and to display this for his information as he passes. It is also very cheap and simple to take an automatic photograph of every car exceeding a predetermined speed, so that its registration number can be read. Clearly such evidence is fair and could be used (though quite properly a period of resistance from the Courts is to be expected).

This is not a very attractive measure upon which to base prosecutions for the reasons given in Section 11.7 below. It is, however, an excellent way of establishing omnipresence quite cheaply, either by making a conspicuous installation; or by an undiscernible installation, whose results are used in approaches to the offenders; or both.

(d) *Conspicuous Observation Boxes*

Conspicuous police observation boxes, which do not show whether or not a policeman is inside, watching, could well contribute to the omnipresence conception. One somewhat unorthodox suggestion is quite hard to fault – that such boxes should be in the shape of oversize policemen.

(e) *Moving Road Blocks*

A great deal can be achieved by inspection points set up by the police and moved from time to time. Even one hour in any one position can make a big impression. Such an activity provides a valuable check on registration, driving licence, condition of vehicle, and so on. Its effect in contributing to the impression of police omnipresence is even more valuable. It is possible to pick out the cases which warrant further inspection by looking at cars while they are held up by traffic lights, and asking only those that seem to call for it to pull into the side. Any impression of officious interruption of a peaceful flow of traffic can thus be avoided.

I understand that a very successful system of this kind operates in Hawaii.

(f) *Propaganda*

Possibly the best yield for money spent on creating omnipresence would be by a publicity drive. This would only be effective if it were not recognized as such.

(g) *Size of Number Plates*

A strong case can be made for increasing the minimum size of number plates to facilitate identification at a distance.

11.6   Borderline Cases

Much emotion is generated by borderline cases. If 30 miles an hour is safe, why is 31 apparently so dangerous? If stopping at a halt sign for one millisecond is all right, why is drifting past it at half a mile an hour so culpable? If a certain percentage of alcohol is respectable, why does another 0.01 % make it so reprehensible? Yet clearly a line has to be drawn, and it can only be quite arbitrary.

There is always a tussle between the administrator and the law giver in such cases. Give us clear statutory guidance and we'll administer it impartially, says the public service. I can't, says the politician, the situation is too complex. I must leave it to you.

The politician sees the unfairness of any hard rules. But in fact rules made by an administration are applied just as blindly as those made by Parliament. No public service, the way we work today, can afford to give discretion to juniors.

Don't worry, says the politician to the public, you can still rely on the top public servants in hard cases. When the obvious untruth of this is pointed out, he offers an appeal to a Member of Parliament or to an Ombudsman. After that, he says, appeal to the courts.

This is crying nonsense. In all such appeals after a fight with the public service, the appellant has arraigned against him all the might and all the rancour of the bureaucrat. There should be only one appeal and only one source of discretion – the courts, who are set up to handle such matters and who have the techniques and experience for it. It is to these that the politicians should hand the discretion, not to the Administration. A man should be able to enter the Courts uncoloured, not a battered combatant after a fight with the bureaucrat.

Very fundamental principles are involved in this. Hayek (Bib. 609, Chapter 6) cites the 'Rule of Law' as one of the greatest achievements of the liberal age. Under it people know where they stand. They know in advance what action the State will take. They know that this action will be impersonal and uncoloured by any special influences. They are then free to arrange their lives within the framework of the law. Hayek, page 81, quotes Kant – 'Man is free if he needs to obey no person but solely the laws'. There can be no liberty without laws.

In striving to reach a set of enforceable statutes, the police all the world over are subscribing to these enlightened ideas. The law should be enforceable and enforced. They are not merely trying to side step the obloquy, and push the unpopular job on to the politicians. The Rule of Law is the only right way, and any other way is indeed the 'road to serfdom'. Any blame in this lies squarely at the door of politicians who are shirking their job.

Once the statutes are clear, a good deal can be done by propaganda, explaining the need to draw an arbitrary line in such cases. Far more important than any explanation, of course, is the rigidity of the rules. Anything completely rigid and well established becomes accepted after a while, and no longer needs explanation (App. 9).

There is much discussion also on the relative importance of different offences. Should infringements of parking rules, or a more or less technical infringement such as not stopping at a Halt sign, be included in any demerit marking system? One school of thought says that the whole Rule of Law is imperilled if some rules are enforced in a half-hearted way. Another school says surely there must be some humanity and common sense in it. Yet parking, apparently such a venial offence, is quite a substantial contributor to traffic accidents. (Smeed, for example, gives it 10%.) The blockage of traffic produces a mood of frustration. The slight pause produced by a true stop provides the 200 millisecond space required for reaction time, and can thus prevent a collision.

There is no adequate answer to this problem. It is a matter of the mood of the community. I suppose it could be said that it is determined by the degree to which the community is in need of intimidation. In a mature and kindly community, truly anxious about traffic accidents, presumably the problem would hardly arise. No mature person feels any loss of status or limitation in obeying the rules of his environment, even if they are a bit unnecessary.

Another intractable problem arises in those countries where speed limits cannot always be enforced, and where as a result unbooked violations run into thousands per motorist per annum (11.2). In such cases the law is cast in the role of an ass and neglecting it clearly does no harm. The community then divides into those who despise it and those who administer it blindly. Motorists get booked for technical breaches of the law with no significance whatever. Demerit marking systems become fiercely unfair. This is considered in the next section, and in more detail in Appendix 11.

11.7 The Esoteric Aspects of Law Enforcement. Speed Limits

If a professor of economics succeeds in discovering how the financial world handles a certain situation and then proceeds to expound on this discovery, the situation immediately changes. For example, where money-making is concerned, when everyone knows the answer, the answer doesn't work any more. The same thing happens in administrative techniques. For example, if a certain method of bringing psychological pressure to bear on executives (which is an essential art of big business) reaches the textbooks, then the executives get to know about it and no longer respond.

The same situation exists with regard to techniques for handling the public. To write about them, or to talk about them, can be a grave disservice, by making the public immune. The policeman's lot in this respect is to listen in silence to much criticism, when all the time there is a perfectly good answer that cannot be given without doing damage.

So it is with speed limits. Speed limits represent a very imperfect rule. They reflect a basically unsound assumption, namely, that, because high speed is dangerous, medium speed must be safe. This is not always so. Under certain conditions there is no safe speed; and there are many conditions when 15 miles an hour is exceedingly dangerous. For example, an impact at 15 m.p.h. is quite enough to do major damage to an elderly pedestrian (see App. 4). Under other conditions – for example a steady stream of cars going down a surburban street – 45 m.p.h. is quite safe. No child will dash out into such a stream. Later in the day, one silent car* at 30 m.p.h. on the same street can be murderous. When the police turn a blind eye to speed limits at 8 a.m. and then enforce them at noon, it may therefore be no weakness, but wisdom. They are landed with an unrealistic legal situation and are making the best of it.

Whatever speed limits exist, a certain proportion of the public will drift up above them. Nor would it be wise to make too much of an issue of this. Driving with one eye on the speedometer can be a dangerous distraction. The present situation in which law is enforced only at whim is not therefore necessarily unsound but may be part of a basic technique, of the kind by which the British achieved such a masterpiece of economic administration in the days of Kipling.

All this is not easily reconciled with Section 11.2, where it was implied that the spectacle of innumerable unpunished violations of speed limits is partly the cause of the public's irresponsible attitude; nor with Section 11.6 where it is said, the mature approach is to modify the laws so that they can be enforced and not place the decision in the hands of officialdom. Surely the 'Rule of Law' is the correct philosophy; not placing everybody completely at the mercy of the bureaucrats' discretion.

We have here the situation described at the start of this section, which cannot be resolved without doing harm. The final policy must be an esoteric and confidential matter, recognized fully perhaps by only a few key officers in the Government and in the police. Sometimes it will be weak and ill thought out; at other times wise and farsighted. But we, the general public, must recognize that the police cannot take us into their confidence. We must be very slow to think we know the answers and could do better.

* We can be grateful that maniacal drivers seem to like noisy exhausts.

This leaves the problem in mid-air. So for those readers who wish to pursue it let us take one typical example of what could be done by the police in an area where the speed limits cannot always be enforced. This I have done in Appendix 11.

11.8   The Separate Traffic Force

Anyone who has lived over a period of years in a community with inadequate traffic patrols is well aware of the increasingly dangerous mood that permeates the roads, until the wildness of driving reaches a pitch where public opinion forces a corrective drive from the police. In such cases the police perforce introduce an intimidatory system without much more than chance operation as to who gets punished, but the public is so relieved that they accept this. Thus a strong attitude in this case produces an improvement. The same attitude in a community which is reasonably well mannered and well disposed towards the police force would have exactly the opposite effect and could well produce no appreciable reduction in traffic accidents at all. In other words, the police are much freer to act where they have no goodwill and no standing than they are when they have achieved a better position. The better the relationship – which one would think would be a favourable condition – the less they can do.

One solution to this is to use a completely separate force, with different uniform and different administrative heads for enforcing traffic law from that used to enforce other law. The antagonism generated by intimidatory tactics applied to a well disposed community is then at least limited more or less to the traffic authorities and should not spread to the enforcement of criminal law as a whole. I have found quite a body of opinion endorsing this.

Many people feel, particularly professional policemen, that it is not possible to keep traffic accidents down to a satisfactory level without a strong measure of intimidation and consequently an inevitable antagonism. There can, for example, be little doubt that this is true when it comes to enforcing parking regulations, and most administrations have created a separate force or at least a separate uniform for this. This is an important point to note, because no one can really dispute the need for parking police and the benefit which they confer on the community as a whole in distributing the available facilities fairly. Yet all those who benefit from this feel no gratitude, and the few greedy ones who are deprived of more than their fair share develop the most astonishing antagonism. 'The meter maids' they call them, and nobody misses a chance to take a crack at them.

Police authorities are sometimes against the separate traffic force (or counting parking – against two separate traffic forces) because there are emergencies when the whole of the police force is needed for other criminal activities and they have to raid the road people for temporary help. One would think that the provision of an extra uniform per man, plus some formality for transferring from one force to the other would not present an insuperable difficulty.

Separate courts for the milder traffic offences have something to be said for them. Using the criminal courts to handle only the truly criminal cases would much lighten the load. See Bib. 612, Napley. I understand such courts, handled by special traffic police wardens, are being used in New Zealand.

11.9 Penalties

Strong theories are held on the type of penalty that should be used in traffic offences.

Monetary fines are universally considered unsatisfactory, as they almost invariably fail to hurt the worst offenders, whilst sometimes representing a major calamity for the milder type of man.

Prison is too tough for all except the most serious motoring offences, if the general public is not to be antagonized.

Withdrawal of licence for varying periods seems to fall most equitably on all shoulders. An adjustment of period in the case of a professional use of the car is clearly something the courts can assess. A particularly interesting suggestion by Napley referred to in Bib. 612 is a postponed withdrawal. This makes possible an extra stage in the application of deterrent pressure.

There is unfortunately often some difficulty in enforcing cancellation of licence. People tend to ignore the disbarment after a while, and if the penalty became general this could easily result in a further deterioration in the status of the police. Willett (Bib. 302) says most motorists in prison in England are there for driving while disqualified. See also Bib. 611.

Impounding the car itself for the period of licence suspension seems the only answer.

CHAPTER 12

Pet Theories

THERE are many pet theories, advanced with complete sincerity, which quite obviously wouldn't work at all. Such things are the suggestions that all cars should be fitted with governors; that the advertising industry should not attempt to appeal to young people by making motoring so glamorous; that everybody should be empowered to arrest dangerous drivers; and so on. Although nearly all these theories have some basis of value, the fact that they wouldn't work in practice is enough to dispose of them.

There is, however, another group that is much more dangerous, because they could be made to work after a fashion. The reason why these theories are so dangerous is that people use them as a kind of alibi. All the effective ways of tackling the accident problem are essentially dreary, dull and unsatisfying. A nice violent move, that satisfies all one's irritations and pent-up resentments, is wonderfully comforting, and allows one to shirk the dull stuff. These are the theories I would like to try to demolish in this chapter.

Many of these theories are clearly the result of a near stampede which is taking place all round the world today, because of the apparent rise in road accidents. It is a great pity that this should happen at a time when, put into perspective, the results are so good. It could easily start a vicious circle, and make things worse again.

With road accidents ten times better than in 1935; with cigarettes said to be killing three or four times as many people as the roads, and with plenty of other far more serious sociological problems, such as the delinquency problems, it is difficult to understand why the politicians have allowed themselves to be so stampeded.

Most pet theory advocates quote some statistics to prove their case. Such statistics are rarely significant; the figures may be correct, but they are not meaningful – they do not establish the conclusions deduced from them. (See App. 5 and Bib. Sect. 7.)

12.1 Stunt Punishments

Nearly all of us assume, quite incorrectly, (11.2), that those who are booked by the police are the ones who cause the accidents. Consequently every so often the newspapers have great fun announcing a new kind of punishment. The offenders should be made to work in the hospitals where the casualties lie and suffer; they should be made to drive with an L badge, to display their disgrace to the world; they should be obliged to attend lectures, film showings, exhibitions of frightful crashes, and so on; they should have 'a governor fitted to their car; they should be made to join discussion groups; and so on.

We have seen in Chapter 11 that the great problem in punishing traffic violations is to persuade the motorist to accept the blame for what he's done. He accepts the punishment – the fine or whatever it may be – without any objections. He sees quite clearly that he's broken the law and has to pay the penalty. But it's quite another matter for him to accept the blame, and see himself in any way at fault. He sees everyone else doing just what he does, and he sees that it is largely a lottery as to who is picked up and who isn't. So the punishment, whatever it may be, does not persuade him to change his thinking; and certainly does not establish the kind of automatic instinctive psychological reaction that we have been searching for throughout this book.

What, then, is achieved by any of these fancy punishments? The answer is that some of them may well enlighten the motorists who are picked up in this way. The advocates of these punishments may justifiably say that whoever is taken along to a hospital, or a wrecker's yard, or whatever it may be, undoubtedly will be a better driver thereafter. But why associate it with a punishment? Isn't this a sure way of starting behind scratch, by bringing in the victim already a little antagonized? As the selection is almost random, would it not be more intelligent to make it obviously random; for example write to representative groups of people and invite them to visit these things as part of some positive drive, not as part of some scheme to punish or humiliate them?

Many of the ideas, such as that of attending lectures or going to hospitals, would involve a good deal of organization and could only handle a very small proportion of the offenders, anyway.

The deterrent effect of these measures would be nil, as is quite clear from the data given in Chapter 11.2. The money which they would cost could be better spent elsewhere. All newspaper editors would do well to add to their 'proscribed' list any stunt punishments for traffic offences.

12.2 Co-opt the Good Drivers

Most of us, when we are subjected to a particularly vicious case of bad driving (which happens every few days) have a great itch to do something about it. Why shouldn't we follow that chap, catch him and arrest him, we say. This is a very understandable instinct, too, because one such maniac can upset us for several hours afterwards, try as we will to remain poised and detached. The importance of educating ourselves and reiterating to ourselves that these wild drivers are not really very dangerous, and do not constitute a major part of the problem, has already been emphasized. Nevertheless, they do produce a good deal of nervous irritation which we could perhaps translate into energy and use. Why shouldn't able motorists of goodwill and integrity be mobilized into a force of special constables, or wardens, of the kind that was so helpful in wartime? Admittedly they would need education, but many of them are not inferior in mental ability to the professionals, and would be quite prepared to take a course of instruction. One would think it would pay the police to make use of all this goodwill, and that it would represent a good financial investment to them.

I do not think any Chief of Police could ever accept such an addition to his staff, no matter how much goodwill was involved.

The reason is one very simple one – that he must have his relationship with the public under his own control. To have people representing him who are not paid by him, and not completely under his control would make his whole job a farce. One could never incorporate such a group of motorists, no matter of how much goodwill, integrity and ability, into the police force. To appreciate this it is necessary to know of the aspects of police work described in Section 11.7.*

Would they have any function as a separate unit? I have never heard a suggestion which would work in regard to this. The public would not readily accept such an uncalled for usurpation of the functions of the police.

It has also been suggested that people who notice very bad driving should report it to the police, with factual information as complete as possible, giving the car registration number of the offender. The police would then send this information on to the offender for comment, and would record it in some sort of a dossier. In the event later on of some major crime being committed by this particular motorist, the dossier would represent a certain amount of supplementary evidence. This scheme appears with many minor variations in nearly all discussions. When you think about it, it is a positively outrageous idea. It is against all principles of justice, with the accused person having the choice of ignoring it, or being put to a great deal of trouble to defend himself, perhaps unnecessarily. Clearly also it would lend itself to grave abuse in the hands of personal enemies.

Nevertheless, rather similar ticket schemes have been introduced in a good many areas, in which an offender is encouraged to pay a fine without attempting to present his case, merely because of the trouble and difficulty it would involve. These schemes are perhaps unavoidable, but they are points of entry to a morass of bad thinking. (See Sect. 11.6.)

All this does seem a pity, because there is a tremendous amount of emotional energy available from people who are annoyed and people who have had trouble from traffic accidents – the distressed and the bereaved. The only constructive use that can be made of this energy is for indignant or distressed people

---

*Also, perhaps, it is not always realized how vital a role is played by the military type of discipline in restraining juniors from abuse of power.

to work it out of themselves by sponsoring discussion groups of the kind advocated in Chapter 6.

The basic answer to the wild and cunning ones is firstly to realize that they are not as bad as they seem, and secondly, the unrecognizable patrol (11.5a).

12.3 Work on Those who have had Accidents

Surely, it is argued, we are justified in the face of such slaughter to take off the road those who have already had a series of accidents? It may be hard on them, but they must be prepared to suffer a little to save a lot. Even if it is largely a chance operation, there is still clear evidence that some improvement would result. (10.4e.)

This argument is only answerable in terms of magnitude. An attempt to assess this by statistical methods is referred to in Bibliography 406. The results are not promising.

Nevertheless, this particular line of thought may well have some value. It may not be strictly justice to penalize the accident repeater, in view of the statistics, but it has that semblance of justice which was considered so important in Chapter 11. The person concerned might well accept it. At least it should be easy to bring enough pressure on him to ensure that he is a willing co-operator, with no tendencies to get the bit between his teeth. I am a little puzzled that no authorities appear to make use of this. Immediately after an accident a man would be very promising material. Perhaps the explanation is that no one knows what to tell him to do (8.3). A suggestion regarding this is given in Appendix 12.

Nor is it clear why one need wait for repeat accidents. One accident is surely sufficient to start clocking up a demerit score. Yet no demerit systems appear to use an accident itself as justifying a mark, possibly because of a quite unjustified assumption that the blame must always lie on one side only. (Chapter 2 indicates that it is to some degree nearly always a joint affair.)

Any action along these lines, however, could only have a secondary effect, which justifies inclusion in the pet theory category.

12.4 Education

One misleading group of theories relates to education. It is the perennial assumption, permeating the whole range of intellectual activity, that education is the answer to just about everything.

We may take as an example the magnificent results of education obtained from groups of drivers by their employers. The results are indubitably impressive. The happy assumption in all the literature that this proves the value of education is not so impressive at all. These men were given something we cannot give to the ordinary motorist – a strong motivation not to run into accidents. This motivation is sufficient to cut vulnerability rate and therefore accident rate quite automatically. As an instance of this consider the youth (3.1) who cut his rate from hundreds a day to nearly nil from the moment he decided he wanted to; and the accident-repeater who stopped completely when he wanted to (11.3).

An employee educational programme provides an excellent motivation – interest, challenge, rivalry, desire to please the boss, wish to clock up a good personal record, desire not to let the team down, and so on. Whether the material taught contributes much remains unproven.

Similarly, it has been clearly demonstrated that those children who obtain a diploma from the school driving course show better accident records than average. Many insurance groups allow them lower premiums. But the successful ones might well be the better types, to whom the kind of thinking involved is congenial, so that they might have had better accident results anyway. An elaborate course, making heavy weather of what to the brighter ones is obvious, could even do harm to some.

We have seen how many doubts arise in connection with the teaching of discipline and morality (9) and we have seen also the many dangers that wrong teaching can lead us into (9.10). We have also seen what unusual and difficult skills in teaching are demanded (9.4 and 9.6).

No one will wish to decry education. But it is no panacea.

The lack of specific evidence for the results of education has been referred to in 9.4.

12.5 Provide an Outlet for Anger

One common suggestion is that there would be an improvement in safety if angry and frustrated motorists could find some outlet. The man who has sat a yard behind another's tail, fuming over what he thinks of as road-hogging, gets some of the annoyance out of his system by cutting in sharply when he finally does pass. Other people hoot belligerently, to let people know that they think they are driving badly.

The uprush of anger in their victims is sometimes quite surprising. I've seen a driver go almost black in the face.

However, no concrete suggestions as to a suitable outlet have emerged.

I have a pet theory of my own here, on a theme at present very much out of fashion. I am convinced that the answer to such situations lies in recovering a sense of style and poise, long since departed from the community. The great discovery of the 'aristocrat' in the days when all people were not equal was that a sense of superiority and detachment, coupled with a certain tinge of contempt and distaste for the ill-behaved, gave tremendous protection and peace of mind. If everybody could see themselves as aristocrats, and could approach the problem with a sense of contempt for the person who gets rattled, it might do a surprising amount of good. But this is still a pet theory. It wouldn't solve the accident problem.

12.6 Use the Girls

One would have thought that girls could have done a great deal to tame youths, and to establish something of a social convention. Surely they could be persuaded to make it plain to the boys that they won't go out with the ones who behave badly on the roads? Surely parents and schools could teach this to the girls, and get it to the point where it was generally accepted.

The answer to this is not promising! The girls are instinctively drawn to wild and adventurous youth. Nor are they necessarily wrong in this. These boys have a spark of something in them that will later take them places. The girls know it, if only subconsciously. It is quite unsound to ask the girls to undertake this civilizing activity (9.2).

This is at first sight a contradiction to the proposals in 9.11 on Teaching an Attitude. Here again the proposals in 9.11 are all right as far as they go. They may do some good. If we pin hopes of any big reduction of accidents from them, except as a small part of a big trend, we make them a pet theory.

12.7 Aunt Sallies: Slow Drivers, Lane Changers, Overtakers

Reference has already been made to the national prejudices – the slow driver in England, the lane changer in America, and the overtaker in France. In Australia it seems to be the high-powered car and the advertising industry. These are not so much pet theories as Aunt Sallies of the moment. I doubt whether anyone seriously thinks that attacking the particular local bugbear will do much to reduce accidents. In each case it is just a reflection of the main local frustration – part of the scenery, so to speak.

12.8 Provisional Licences and Labels

It is often pointed out that drivers who have just passed their tests are not yet fully skilled. Perhaps they should carry a label, so that other drivers can be warned, and also can give more patience. It is also said frequently that such beginners should receive extra scrutiny, and any tendency to careless driving punished with quick withdrawal of their licence. It is felt that the full licence should not be granted until a period of trouble-free driving has passed.

Such measures are advocated mostly with young people in mind and they are in line at first sight with the recommendation of 9.2 – get tough with youths – but with a difference. In 9.2 it was said 'Get tough with youths who drive dangerously.' We must beware that this does not become 'get tough with youths for being young.' They should not, merely because they are young, be subject to a worse-than-average penalty. In fact youth is entitled to a little extra patience while it is learning and must not be bullied. (App. 16).

We have seen in Chapters 2 and 11 that any penalization based on violations or on accidents would operate as a matter of chance and would not pick the wicked ones. To make violations or accidents therefore a justification for labelling young people, and suggesting to them that they are worse-than-average drivers would be grossly unfair. (Except on a demerit marking system involving at least four marks.) It certainly, also, would be completely ineffective. It could easily make young people of good intent over-anxious, and produce more rather than less accidents. It would make a great barrier to that confident, easy approach which I have called the positive mood (see Chapter 9) and which makes all the difference to the ease of learning, and the degree of skill achieved.

Such schemes, I think, are the product of over-anxiety on the part of the authorities.

12.9 Multiple Speed Limits

The speed that could be presumed safe on a dry road should not be permitted on a wet or frozen road. A speed that is safe uphill is not safe downhill. A speed that is safe on a new car with efficient braking may be very unsafe with an older car or a car in bad condition. It has been suggested, for example, that all speed limits should be twofold, say 30/40, or 40/50, the higher speed being permissible only with new cars, not downhill, on a dry day.

It seems improbable that any of these measures would be effective. The considerations put forward in Section 11.7 indicate that they would be administratively unsound. The considerations in Chapter 9 indicate that they might do more harm than good, by exaggerating the function of arbitrary rules.

Multiple speed limits have been introduced rather successfully, to slow down traffic on holiday periods. Stretches of roads are equipped with special 50 m.p.h. limit signs that are exposed only for week-ends and holidays.

There could also be much in favour of a similar top speed limit (perhaps 50 m.p.h.) for night driving. There is surprisingly little data available on whether accidents are more likely in darkness (see, however, Bib. 309). It is difficult to observe all vulnerabilities in darkness, so that this could perhaps be a more significant point than is generally realized. The combination of darkness and extreme tiredness could be extremely dangerous. However, in the absence of data, this can only be classed as a pet theory also.

12.10 Ban Over-powered Large Cars

Time (12th June, 1964) reports that in Illinois small cars kill twice as many people as big ones. This could prove anything. If the corpses are in the small cars it suggests how dangerous are the large ones. If the corpses are on the road it suggests how dangerous are the small ones.

Basically, the heavier the car, the safer. The driver of a large car is unlikely to suffer much personal damage by collision with a light car. Nor is he so likely to be forced off the road or into other troubles.

Large powerful cars generally have careful drivers and would probably show up statistically as better than average. Yet with a wild driver they are clearly more dangerous. Given one car in ten as overpowered, 2% wild drivers, and each wild driver producing 5 times average vulnerability, the decrease in the 'cloud of threats' (see Chapter 2) by banning all big cars would be maximum $\frac{1}{10} \times 2\% \times 5$, i.e. a 1% reduction in accidents. 1% is well worth having, but it is not a *major* contribution to the problem, as so many people believe.

There is clear evidence from research (Bib. 15) that, statistically, high-powered cars are not more dangerous at all, but that low-powered cars are decidedly more dangerous than average. This is probably because low power means long vulnerabiliites and high power short ones.

12.11 Ban the Aged Driver

There is a certain amount of statistical evidence that aged

drivers have more accidents (Bib. 1, pp. 118–25). This is far from conclusive. Insurance statistics show little to support the idea. There is a strong and widespread prejudice against the aged drivers, particularly among professional drivers and police. This tendency to blame the old driver would itself be enough to explain the statistics. Certainly there is insufficient evidence to support the pet theorists, some of whom go so far as to advocate banning all drivers over 60.

My investigations indicate that older people tend to become over aware of road dangers and give up driving long before they need. Those older drivers I observed show as good vulnerability rates as any. I think the prejudice against old drivers arises from the basic misunderstanding of the nature of collisions which I have endeavoured to correct in Chapter 2. 'Of course he must be more dangerous,' they say, 'he's slowing up and his faculties are deteriorating.' This is a complete *non sequitur*. The influence of most of these deteriorating faculties will be negligible.

The most potentially dangerous group of older people would be those whose mental powers are deteriorating. Any re-testing of old drivers should concentrate on this.

12.12 Pet Causes of Accidents

Much effort has been spent on endeavouring to determine causes of accidents. North-Western University (Bib. 4) gives detailed guidance for Investigating Officers.

The statistics give valuable information, but are frequently difficult to use because of the demand for one main explanation per accident; i.e., the percentages for the different causes are made to add up to 100. There are probably few major accidents with less than four or five contributory causes. If all these causes were given due weight, the returns would look something like this:

Cause	Operative in % of accidents		
	Light	*Serious*	*Fatal*
Inattention (at least 1 driver)	100	100	100
Alcohol (at least 1 driver)	20	40	50

Cause	Operative in % of accidents		
	Light	Serious	Fatal
Imperfection in equipment	20	30	40
Unsafe roads	100	100	100
Offside turns	25	20	15
Jumping Traffic Lights	20	15	10
Failure to yield	15	20	25
At least 1 driver in a hurry	60	80	90
At least 1 driver with the bit between his teeth (the hard core)	50	90	90
Failure of automatic pilot (at least one driver)	30	80	80

and so on.

All drivers and all except the most highly-trained observers give wrong information about accidents. A driver who knows he is culpable starts a process of re-telling within minutes of the crash. After a day or so he is sincerely convinced of the truth of his story – often a most astonishing perversion of the facts.

Statistics prove irrefutably that the main cause of accidents is whatever the investigators believe it to be – speed, drinking, inattention, bad roads, driver psychology or what you will. How can it not be speed, when obviously the accident wouldn't have happened if someone had not been going too fast? How can it not be alcoholism when most drivers drink some alcohol? Or not bad roads, when the accident clearly wouldn't have happened if the traffic engineering had been safe enough? Or not inattention, which must nearly always operate; and so on.

There are certain statistics that give clear leads. For example, the Paris results show that the physical state of the driver is the cause of less than 2% of collisions; or the New York figures show that 35% of those who died were intoxicated (clear deductions regarding the effect of alcohol in these areas may be drawn, though even in these cases they may not be what the reader expects (see 12.13)). As another example: all police statistics show a fair proportion of accidents associated with an off-side turn. Clearly an off-side turn is a vulnerable manoeuvre for many drivers.

The analysis of these causes and the resulting action is part of the complex network of professional activities described in

10.1; the relative importance of the different causes is clearly a local affair, and a matter to be determined by the judgement of men who have the local picture at their fingertips.

Almost any generalization on the cause of traffic accidents therefore can be regarded as a pet theory and discounted.

12.13 Alcohol

Research has clearly demonstrated the adverse effect of alcohol on many driver characteristics. Research has also demonstrated that the effect of the deterioration in such characteristics on the probability of accidents is not very significant. Most drivers make allowance for such defects when they are permanent, but there is no evidence as to how much they allow for temporary deterioration. It could well be that up to a point alcohol does little harm. The difficulty lies in deciding what this point is (as in other borderline cases considered in 11.6). Clearly a definition must be made, and no one should object if it is set on the safe side. The attempts to get simple test methods accepted and a clear definition written into the law, are worthy of the most vigorous support.

The situation is vastly different in different communities. The statistical report of the City of New York Police Department for 1963 (p.7) says 'of all persons over 16 years of age who died within twenty-four hours of an accident, 38% of the drivers and 33% of the pedestrians were intoxicated'. Also, from the same report: 'an intensified year-long drive, initiated to reduce accidents, resulted in 4,508 arrests for drinking-driving . . . In 3,013 cases, persons arrested were taken into custody for drinking-driving while in full flight, before an accident could occur.' From the foregoing can be deduced that intoxication was a factor in New York City in less than 2% of the 58,000 killed and injured, and this is confirmed by the detailed statistics. The situation in Paris is much the same, and in London the percentage is even lower.

The point emphasized by Moseley (Bib. 206) of the fundamental difference between injury and fatality accidents, explains the apparent contradiction in the foregoing. As a factor in violent accidents alcohol deserves to be taken seriously; as a factor in accidents as a whole it is not, in many areas, a major item.

This is perhaps confirmed for U.K. by the Ministry of Transport figures (quoted by Robert Glenton, Sunday Express, 5th January, 1964) (116/110) for serious or fatal accidents 1963: Intoxicated 432, Learners 5,622, Offside turn 11,405, Lost control 16,708.* These conclusions also appear to be confirmed by the results of the Christmas period 1964, after the campaign against alcohol referred to in Section 6.2. There was some indication of reduction in fatalities but none in the total number of accidents.

Police and ambulance men tell some horrific stories of vomiting drunks staggering around helplessly amongst the carnage they have caused, and yet escaping punishment for a variety of reasons. A long time elapses before a doctor sees them; they sober up quickly under the impact of the accident; the doctor makes pedantic reservations in his evidence before the Court; the defence exploits the reluctance of the jury by making much of any such reservations; so that quite a number of scandalous cases escape completely. Our reaction to this is rather like our reaction to the wild driver, who outrages us so that we see him as more important than he is, and feel that every attempt must be made to catch him and punish him. There is, as we have said before, absolutely nothing wrong with this feeling, provided we don't let it unbalance our picture of the situation as a whole. No one would assert that drinking is a negligible factor. It becomes a pet theory if we allow it to distract us from more vital measures, which would have a more significant result. For example, even a very limited vulnerability drive would pay at least ten times the dividend that all the efforts on drinking can yield. (10% as compared with 1%.)

There are some areas, notably Los Angeles and New South Wales, where the statistics indicate that alcohol is a much bigger factor than those given above for New York, London and Paris. Los Angeles gives 8.8% (1963 Statistical Digest p. 62), and New

---

*'The Times' quotes Ministry of Transport figures for 1964 of 7,820 and 95,460 for fatal and serious accidents, quoting 13% and 9% increase on 1963. One can work for months on reconciling such figures without profiting at all.

South Wales gives Accidents 5·5%, Deaths 7.9% (1963 Police
Report p. 7). The N.S.W. figures seem to indicate more than
double the proportion of cases of driving while under the
influence of alcohol compared with New York.

Alcohol is to be seen as part of the problem which is catered
for, perhaps even a little disproportionately, in the network of
official activity going on in all countries. The authorities are
prepared to go to endless trouble to make small reductions
wherever they can find them, the effectiveness of which is often
hard to prove. Their reward lies in the truly remarkable overall
picture of Chapter 1 (a 10: 1 improvement in thirty years) to
which we have had to refer so frequently.

12.14 Road Engineering

Road engineering is another one of these endless unrewarding
detailed activities described in 10.1, the overall result of which
is so successful. Like alcohol, its effect on accidents as a whole is
probably quite different from its effect on fatalities. Speeding
up the flow of traffic and removing obstructions reduces the
number of collisions; those collisions which do occur, being at a
higher speed, tend to be more serious.

The differences between town and country in this sphere
are significant. In towns the speeds still do not rise to anything
excessive, so that a reduction in accidents can be achieved by
road engineering without any price to pay. Out in the country,
road engineering is more of a mixed blessing. The speed steps
up. Some of the accidents on high-speed motorways, although
rare, are truly fearsome.

This is reflected in the statistics. Most countries as a whole
show about double the number of fatalities, related to population of that achieved in the big cities.

The effect of eliminating parking from city streets and from
narrow country roads, which acts to improve flow, is found to have
a remarkable effect on accident rate. Smeed (10.1 and Bib. 3)
estimates 10% improvement in accidents by this means alone.

Road engineering is, of course, a full-time professional
activity, with its own magazines, technical bodies, conferences,
etc., and is the basis for a large industry. There is a steady trend

in it towards better flow paths, safer crossings, greater segregation, better lighting, better traffic signals at intersections, co-ordination between signals at successive intersections, and so on. All this calls for no comment in the present study.*

Road engineering becomes a pet theory when, as so frequently happens, it is used as a stick to beat the authorities. Diatribes about the amount of money collected from motorists and not spent on the roads may well have some basis; but not to the point of putting the whole accident situation on to this aspect. Fifty millions spent on this would give less result than fifty thousand spent on an 'observe your vulnerabilities' drive.

12.15   Stiffer Driving Tests. Repeat Tests

It is surely logical that people's driving ability should be carefully scrutinized before they are allowed on the roads.

The aspects of a would-be driver's suitability that lend themselves to examination are: firstly, his ability to handle the vehicle (9.6); secondly, his knowledge of the working rules of traffic tactics (9.4); and thirdly, his ability to detect vulnerabilities. There seems little doubt that until he can satisfy an examiner on these points, he should not be allowed on the roads.

There seems no way of determining by examination those qualities that lead to accidents. So many factors in his make-up determine the risks he will take. Even if any psychological tests could be evolved they would be largely vitiated by the presence of the examiner. This alone creates too different an environment. The cunning ones are passed, the anxious ones rejected. Yet the anxious ones could well be the safer.

The foregoing places a definite limit on what can be achieved

---

*One is tempted sometimes to wonder how it is possible that such shocking street lighting installations continue to be made. Why it was ever necessary to set up lights which shine in motorists' eyes I have never been able to discover. One would have thought that a hooded reflector was one of the cheapest and most efficient devices available, yet the number of street lights in which the bare light is still visible from a car is staggeringly high. This does not seem to be the fault of the manufacturers, who advertise proper fittings and show photographs of streets lit without a single lamp directly visible. Over the last thirty years I have asked Municipal Authorities for an explanation of this, but have never been able to get an answer.

by stiffer driving tests. Even in the realm where these tests are useful, too much emphasis on secondary matters can do harm, by conveying the impression that the rules are the whole story, and by making the rules too sacrosant (9.3). The matter, like the educational problem as a whole, should be approached with diffidence. The likelihood that any great improvement in accidents can be achieved by a stiffening or changing of driving tests seems to be remote indeed, other than perhaps by placing more emphasis on ability to detect vulnerabilities.

Quite a deal of attention is paid at present in most driving examinations on ability to detect vulnerabilities, although perhaps this phrase is not used. Examiners do look for a driver's awareness of the possible dangers in the situation before him.

Assuming the driving tests are realistic, and not preoccupied with secondary rules, then it is difficult at first sight to find any objection to the plea that after any accident or any citation a motorist should submit to them again before being allowed on the roads. Unfortunately, so many examiners do develop little shibboleths and foibles which in practice would make this extremely unfair on the older driver. In some areas success in the driving test really depends on knowing a series of little tricks. These get passed around among the young people, but the mature motorist might be quite unaware of them. Theoretically, the repeat test seems in line with our conclusions regarding the need to intimidate. Nevertheless, as things are in most countries today, I would have grave doubts about its wisdom. A great deal more work on the training and the control of the examiners is necessary before this could be advocated with confidence. (Bib. 208, 215.)

It was claimed recently in England that the ratio of passes to failures varies as much as four to one from one examination centre to another. This is tantamount to proof that the present examination system is no adequate mechanism.

CHAPTER 13

Where Do We Now Stand?

13.1 The Ultimate Objective

THE ultimate objective is that we should live together on the
road as we do today on the sidewalks, without ever dreaming
of doing violence to each other. There will then be no more
accidents on the roads than there are now on the sidewalk.

Two hundred years ago the risks of walking around were
probably at least as bad as the risks of driving around today.
There was a fair chance of being knifed or clubbed or blud-
geoned, and quite a likelihood of being shouldered out of the
way by passing bullies. No doubt there were shoving priorities,
like pecking priorities in a hen run, or shouting down priorities
as exist in many men's clubs today. (A is permitted to shove or
peck or shout down everyone, B everyone except A, and so on,
while everybody does it to poor Z.) Probably before police
patrols were introduced the suggestion that going out for a
walk could ever be safe would, in many places, have seemed
preposterous.

It is interesting to observe that with the abandonment of the
police beat system recently in many places, the tendency for
toughs to bully their way along the sidewalk is returning, and
the tally of brutal assaults is rising again.

The suggestion that we can abolish road accidents entirely
is nearly always treated with ridicule, chiefly on the grounds
that the speeds and risks make it impossible. Yet such an argument is itself ridiculous, when in spite of the speeds and risks
the average man drives for thirty years per crash.

It seems likely that we find ourselves today at about the same
stage as met Sir Robert Peel last century. Everyone says it can't
be done. Yet I have asked many people how many accidents
would there be if every time a case of bad driving occurred

a police car immediately took off after it and halted the offending motorist. The answer, given after much hesitation, is nearly always: hardly any!

Of course there must be a period of adjustment. I have no doubt that the early Peelers had a torrid time establishing their omnipresence.

How hard it is going to be and how long it will take depends on the extent to which we can induce a co-operative mood in the general public. This is what we have been chiefly considering in this book. Yet all the measures proposed will never take us to the ultimate objective of fewer accidents unless they are supplemented by a step-up in police activity. This surely needs no expounding. The tough, the drunk, the wild man will always be with us.

A step-up in police activity will be equally ineffective without the other measures advocated. Especially will it be defeated if we fail to induce a general mood of better temper and courtesy, such as to highlight the antisocial few, and separate them off from the body of decent people. Rough behaviour on the sidewalk today is immediately obvious and quickly meets retribution because of its isolation and conspicuousness.

The very first requirement is that all road users should behave with courtesy, good temper and care. We must all give a lead in this direction. No one in authority, and no private individual, no matter what the provocation, should do or say anything whatever to encourage either fear or anger. We must of course treat antisocial individuals with proper sternness. But we should not start a persecution by inveighing against classes or groups, whether women drivers, youths or drunks; not seek violent punishments or revenge; not make violent pronouncements about motorists being criminals, fatal accidents being murder, wild youths needing to be wildly punished. Such talk (although perhaps partly justifiable) is unwise, unhelpful, and administratively speaking, basically unsound. He who would inculcate self-restraint must surely show it in his own bearing. People who have accidents may be unskilled, unwise, unlucky or unrestrained. But, with few exceptions, they do not *seek* accidents. They are not like burglars. They gain nothing by having accidents. Any one of us who sounds off so virtuously against these people can, any day, find himself or his son in dock amongst them.

We should all, also, inform ourselves of the facts and think out the rights and wrongs of the situation. Some of us, finding a ticket, even curse the parking police, whose only activity is to see that we all get a fair share of the available space. How feeble-minded can we get!

Finally we must all fight our own anger. If someone behaves badly this gives us no right to be angry. We are not Zeus sitting in judgement on the sins of others from the throne of our own purity.

The need to avoid inflaming the resentments and setting us at each other's throats does not imply any obligation to shut our eyes to realities. We know there are shocking cases of wild youths, drunks, etc. We must not oversimplify our approach. The policeman who is benign and patient with the naughty small boy must become a tiger when he spots the criminal. It is sometimes a nice point of judgement to know which is which.

13.2 The Need for Re-Appraisal

The virtuous principles given in the foregoing paragraphs will be approved by all. But nothing will change as a result. Why is this? I hope I have succeeded in demonstrating the answer in the foregoing chapters. It is because of the almost complete wrongness of current thinking. Nearly every man greatly over-estimates his driving skill; blames the other fellow; has a pet theory which, as an effective measure, is always unsound; feels entitled to get angry; feels absolutely no call to do anything himself. Most propaganda is unsound because it implies that some abnormality produces the accidents (drinking, speed, etc.) and thus confirms this general smugness of attitude of the ordinary motorist.

This general attitude prevents any adequate action by the police, because of the intensity of indignation which such action arouses. It creates widespread nervous and anxious driving – an effect which is going to become more and more damaging as the lack of self-confidence being induced in youth gets carried over into the body of adult motorists. It blocks completely any attempt to get the average driver to step up his safety margin.

A small proportion of motorists are reachable in these matters. They will read books like this one, they keep an open mind, and are prepared to accept the proposition that not everything in life is amenable to simplification down to one sentence.

The bulk of motorists are quite out of reach. Ordinary propaganda channels will carry only lightweight ideas. The whole principle of public relations depends on plugging endlessly one, or at most two, simple sentences. Even this sometimes takes years to penetrate. The problem in the present case is not merely to convey one or two simple ideas, but first to destroy a whole group of basic assumptions, many of them quite unconscious, which present a complete blockage. While a motorist is convinced that the wild drivers he sees are the cause of accidents, and that someone else is responsible, not he, he is hardly likely to accept a complex set of reasoning on quite a different basis, such as is necessary to get him to count his vulnerabilities. Similarly, while he is convinced that the police operate primarily to collect revenue, that they don't go after the real offender, and that they only make citations during the part of the day that suits them, he is not ready to be persuaded that an increase in citations would actually present a step-up in fairness.

This problem is a major sociological one. It is not like teaching a student, prepared to listen. It is rather like conveying the elements of modern chemistry to a mediaeval alchemist, who not only wouldn't listen but would consider that the nonsense he had accumulated in a lifetime's study justified him in knowing better than his would-be teacher. There is general agreement that no channel exists today whereby this kind of fundamental reassessment can be made to happen in the ordinary mind.

This is not at all the same thing as educating a man, or bombarding him with a series of very simple propositions, as in high-powered public relations work. Nor is it a matter of exhortation as practised by reform movements and churches. The problem is to make him think about these matters for himself.

Years ago there were several ways in which this could be approached. Many novels incorporated a good deal of subtle social propaganda and careful discussion. Many newspaper articles did the same. There was a habit of conversation in much of the ruling community, and the less sophisticated people had no say. Nowadays various pressures have completely changed the position. For example, television places a great premium on a superficial and specious approach. Analysis of the facts, careful weighing of the data, in fact any kind of complexity, results in loss of part of the audience.

Moreover, there are nowadays more matters competing for attention. Many of them are worrying. We don't like to think about them. We get a habit of rejecting any anxious discussion. The pseudo-expert, who specializes in reassurance and a good façade, is such a comfort that we want to believe him and to discount any objective man who makes us anxious. The knowledgeable man, always diffident and tentative, gets less of a hearing than ever. This is further accentuated by the fact that increasing complexity makes it more difficult for us to judge for ourselves. It takes more time to discover the true position, just when we have less time to devote to it.

The press must perforce play along with this demand for simplification. If it prints a balanced picture, detailed enough to be useful, it will not be read. This is doubly true in matters such as road accidents, because the right conclusions are so unpalatable, so dull, and sheet the responsibility so directly home to the reader himself.

The solution proposed in Chapter 6 to this sociological difficulty – that of small discussions – is a general one applying not merely to traffic accidents but to most other social problems – problems of government, of defence, deviant behaviour by adolescents, increase in crime, deterioration of morality and many others, all of which are becoming increasingly urgent. The proposition is quite specific. It is that security plus affluence results in degeneration and only a conscious attempt at self-discipline can replace the automatic discipline of harder times. A machine for creating such conscious discipline in our community has to be built from scratch. None exists. The only mechanism which can be used is general thinking, promoted by general discussion. True discussion, as distinct from lecturing, can only take place in small groups.

There may be other solutions. This is the only one that I have been able to uncover. Such as it is, it has the support of almost all the experts with whom it has been discussed.

It is, of course, a long-dated project. This should not discourage us, as it is generally conceded that it takes 20 to 25 years to establish any basic new idea in the community. If we can get some results in an appreciably shorter period than this, our efforts will have been more than worthwhile.

13.3   The Re-Appraisal Society

I had seen this need for a new social mechanism earlier, in several other sociological investigations. There was, however, one striking difference between the road accident problem and all the others. This I have described in Chapter 7. It is the general interest and readiness to talk.

I began to wonder whether this general interest might not be the opportunity I had been long searching for. It might give a favourable starting point for the new mechanism. I tried the idea out on many friends in England, U.S.A. and Australia, with by no means discouraging results, and we finally decided to set up the Re-Appraisal Society. Road accidents were made its first project.

I hope that many of my readers will feel impelled to join in this very modest adventure. If it 'takes' and becomes self-energizing it might be very valuable. At its worst, it offers a pleasant and amusing hobby, that can take as little or as much time as circumstances demand.

13.4 Action

The Re-Appraisal Society aims only to get people thinking. The conclusions they reach are relatively of secondary importance. In fact, there may be many social problems where the best line of attack is still quite obscure. In the case of road accidents, however, as I hope this book has demonstrated, there are certain things which could be advocated with reasonable certainty. Here they are, with references to the appropriate sections.

(a) *What Should the Ordinary Man Do about Road Accidents?*
    (i)   Cultivate visual perception (2.1 and 9.9).
    (ii)   Observe his driving, particularly when tired, angry or in a hurry. Instal a counter on the dashboard and measure his vulnerabilities (3.6), and thus reduce his chances of serious injury from 1 in 4 to 1 in 40.
    (iii) Put all pet theories into perspective (12).
    (iv) Refuse, as far as possible, to get angry, to be rushed, to drive when tired, or after alcohol (10).
    (v)   Avoid inflammatory talk (13.1).
    (vi) Support the police, the safety authorities, educational schemes and road improvements as vigorously as possible (10.1).
    (vii) Get well informed on the whole subject, and discuss it with friends in order to get them thinking about it (6.5). The Re-Appraisal Society offers itself to help in this.

(b) *What Should the Authorities Do?*
    (i)   Back the three Es: Enforcement, Education, Engineering (10.1). In particular, step up road patrols; work on police omnipresence; work on improving the fairness of any delicensing system in use (11).
    (ii)   Start a vulnerability drive (5.2).
    (iii) Investigate new ideas such as the push-button brake (App. 1) and modified insurance legislation (11.3).
    (iv) Ignore pet theories (12).
    (v)   Get tougher with the young (9). Yet at the same time, get gentler with the young (9.2, 11.4, 12.8). The task of breaking in the colt without damaging him is a delicate one We are making errors both by inadequate punishment of bad cases and by creating unnecessary anxieties in the ordinary young person. We may easily damage the driving ability of the next generation (Bib. 303).
    (vi) Avoid inflammatory talk and violent measures (13.1).

(c) *What Should the Newspapers, Magazines and Broadcasters Do?*
    (i)   Avoid inflammatory talk (13.1), pet theories (12),

suggestions of stunt punishments and violent measures (12.1).

(ii)   Avoid glib pronouncements that sound good or novel, but which are not based on adequate knowledge. The Re-Appraisal Society offers itself to provide data, and to put writers in touch with experts and authorities.

(iii) Give as much support as possible to the various measures indicated throughout this book.

PART III

Miscellaneous Points

The appendices that follow and the remarks in the
Bibliography are mostly as significant as the main text.
They were separated out only because they would
have interfered in the line of reasoning.

They are not arranged in any logical sequence.

APPENDIX 1

The Push-Button Brake

Stunts and gadgets are nearly always disappointing. The wise man is slow to advocate them. There is, however, one gadget that properly used could make a sensational reduction in accidents, and do even more to reduce the amount of damage when accidents do occur.

Like all such measures – for example, better roads or seat belts – it will be largely defeated in the long run by motorists relying on it to justify harder driving and thus moving back to their old vulnerability rate. But combined with an adequate campaign on vulnerability it could make a substantial contribution to safety.

This gadget is the push-button brake.

The average time required to respond to a visual stimulus by taking the foot off the accelerator and putting it on the brake is 700 to 800 milliseconds. The average time required to press a button in response to a visual stimulus is 200 to 300 milliseconds. The response time by the hand to a knock on the hand can be as low as 25 milliseconds. Thus in one step the greater part of the most vital danger period can be eliminated.

Many drivers already use this principle to some degree. They instinctively hold their foot poised above the brake pedal whenever they take it off the accelerator pedal. This halves their response time.

There is surely no need to expound on the effectiveness of this. At 60 m.p.h. it means that the free run distance, from when the danger is perceived to when the brakes begin to be applied, will be reduced from 66 feet to 22 feet. The free run distance for a car hit unexpectedly, and careering across the traffic stream – the chief cause of multiple accidents – will be reduced to a few feet, as the brake will be applied by direct muscle reaction to the jerk, not by reaction to a visual stimulus.

The push button should be in the form of a ring on the upper side of the steering-wheel. It must operate in addition to, not instead of, the foot brake.

The reason why this has not yet been used, I suppose, is that it has dangers unless the driver wears a seat belt. His other bodily reactions would not keep pace with the brake and he would be jerked forward.

In the ideal arrangement the push-button brake would probably be combined with a clampable seat belt, that normally allows freedom of movement up to a certain point, but which takes up all free length of belt. The application of the push-button brake would then automatically cause clamping of the seat belt.

If it were felt that the use of seat belts could never be relied on, there would still be a substantial gain available by arranging for the automatic part of the brake application to apply graduated pressure – a light pressure at the moment of reaction growing to full pressure in the following, say, 200 milliseconds. Such devices can now be produced with complete reliability, and at low cost.

The push-button brake must, of course, automatically cut the engine throttle, because the driver's jerk forward could operate to depress the accelerator.

Anyone who doubts the efficacy of this should try it out on any one of the response-time testing machines, now available in most cities. With his foot poised above the brake pedal, he will find his response time is indeed about half of what it is when he starts with his foot depressing the accelerator. A further reduction to about one third is achieved when the hand is used to press a button.

Cars equipped with a push-button brake would need to carry a sign similar to that carried by vehicles with air-brakes. Something such as 'Push-button brake. Please keep well away from my tail'.

The operation of the push-button brake would need to light up a vivid sign at the rear of the car – something in addition to the normal red light.

The reader will readily appreciate the extreme significance of the response time of 25 milliseconds which can be obtained from the hand in response to muscular or tactile stimulus. Most corrective steering, e.g. response to a lurch, is carried out in this manner, not by response to a visual stimulus. I discovered this during the second war when we built a remote controlled motor-car in an endeavour to find some means of defending Australia. There were virtually no aeroplanes or guns or any other means of carrying an adequate amount of fire power to the enemy at the time. We decided that the only available carrying device was the ordinary motor-car, and we made a plan to commandeer 10,000 or so of these, reinforce them with hardwood, load them with explosives, and use them as projectiles to be driven by remote control against an invasive force. At this distance this may sound a little wild, but at the time it was by no means foolish. One American general, in a position to judge, commended it very generously.

When we built this car and drove it up and down the roads of Sydney (probably breaking every possible traffic regulation), we found it extremely difficult to steer with any accuracy. For a long while we thought it was our control mechanism but we finally established that many minor steering corrections are made in response to the lurching of the car and not to a visual observation. The muscles of the body and the hand observe the impact of any movement either from the car itself or from the steering-wheel, and react to it from subcentres in the nervous system, not from the brain. We ended up by working out remote control systems in which the 'feel' of the controls was signalled back to the operator.

APPENDIX 2

One-Man Accidents

Accidents described as 'vehicle/object' or 'vehicle runs off the road' are strikingly on the increase in many areas. They were, until recently, rarely more than 10% but are now often up to 20%.

The probability structure of such accidents is surely simpler than for collisions. Almost certainly the likelihood of such an accident would be immediately related to the number of vulnerabilities. A sudden upsurge of vulnerabilities would be a clear warning. Motorists who have to make very long journeys alone therefore, could benefit greatly by adopting the vulnerability observation techniques set out in this book.

The question of the cause of the increase in these accidents is of profound importance. Much research is going on. There seems little doubt that one cause is increased drug taking. Deterioration of mechanical service standards is another. Diminution of the aspiration towards physical fitness, as part of the current cult of degeneracy, is a third. As so often, the problems of the accident relate directly back to the problems of Society as a whole.

APPENDIX 3

Estimate of Confrontation Frequency*

Assume a vulnerability lasts on the average 1 second.

Assume a driver drives 1 hour ($= 3,600$ secs.) a day, makes 10 vulnerabilities, and meets 500 other cars.

Assume that all drivers whom he meets make 10 vulnerabilities each.

Then he is vulnerable for 10 seconds out of 3,600 – that is, for $\frac{1}{360}$ of the time that he is driving. When he meets another car, the vulnerability of its driver will coincide with his own for $\frac{1}{360} \times \frac{1}{360}$ of his driving time. That is, there will be a confrontation with this driver for this fraction. As, by assumption, he meets 500 other drivers, the average number of confrontations per day will be $\frac{1}{360} \times \frac{1}{360} \times 500$. In a year of 365 days the average number will be $\frac{1}{360} \times \frac{1}{360} \times 500 \times 365 = 1.41$.

*I am indebted to Mr. G. F. O'dell for this presentation.

This calculation is intended only to show the order of magnitude of the occurrence of confrontations; for instance, it does not take account of the variation of the duration of a confrontation from 1 second, when the vulnerabilities of two cars begin just when they meet, to zero, when the vulnerability of either car is just ended at the time of meeting.

Then, too, it does not bring out that the frequency of confrontations may be much increased during periods of icy roads or in the difficult half-hour between sunset and lighting-up time.

Again, when one car is overtaking another, the duration of a confrontation may be much greater than usual.

Roads restricted in one direction present an entirely separate problem.

APPENDIX 4

Dangerous Speeds (*Elaboration of 10.7*)
To get the effect of running into a stationary truck at 15 m.p.h. picture a concrete floor with your steering wheel stuck into it by its column, projecting about a foot. Imagine yourself lying face down on the floor with your stomach draped over the steering wheel. Four very large men pick you up by your arms and legs and raise you in the air until you are suspended horizontally $7\frac{1}{2}$ feet up. Then they let go and you fall spread-eagled on to the wheel and the concrete. If you think glass might be kinder to your face than concrete, there's no objection to putting a sheet of glass on the floor to represent the windscreen; or add any other of the dash fittings in the appropriate positions.

Those who feel they could protect themselves with their hands and arms in a crash should try to visualize to what a limited degree they could break their fall under the above conditions. The forces and masses are strictly comparable in the two cases, and the hands and arms are not nearly strong enough to provide any protection except as a piece of padding.

A pedestrian hit by your car at 15 m.p.h. gets approximately the same impact that you yourself would receive in the above case.

To get the effect of hitting the stationary truck at 30 m.p.h. do the same thing, except that you are raised 30 feet up (rooftop of a two-storey house) before they let you drop on to the wheel. For 60 m.p.h. the distance is 120 feet – say the 14th floor of an apartment building.

To get the effect of a safety belt, picture one of these on strong supports slung just above the wheel to break your fall.

This analogy explains rather vividly why, after you have helped get the spokes of a broken steering-wheel out of a corpse's stomach, you tend to drive slowly for a while, and become irritable when someone talks of 'just crawling along, my dear, at 45'.

APPENDIX 5

The Significance of Statistics

Much misunderstanding derives from an inability to discern the true significance of certain statistics. We may take as a typical example of this a letter published in *Time*, Pacific edition, 26th February, 1965, in which a reader announced with joy that he had at last found the statistical proof he had been looking for for years as to the value of seat belts: of thirty-four people killed on the New Jersey Turnpike in the last year not one was wearing a seat belt. This to him was proof. It is of course equally proof that feather boas are very safe for motorists, because not one of those thirty-four wore a feather boa. The real significance of the figure cannot be determined until one knows what proportion of the motorists on the New Jersey Turnpike was wearing a seat belt. If this were nil, then the proof is nil. If this were a high proportion, then the proof is on its way. It would still not be certain as it could well be that people who wear seat belts also drive more carefully.

As a result of this I spent a couple of hours observing cars on the New Jersey Turnpike. I saw one driver only with a harness and none with belts visible. A bus driver on the route estimated that less than 10% wear belts.

Typical of this type of statistic is the lung cancer information, and all the information on accidents related to causes or to driver characteristics. Millions of observations may be taken, but the proof is still missing. There are too many factors involved, and it is a matter of opinion always as to which are significant and which are not.

At the other end of the scale we have statistics of the kind used in production sampling tests. Suppose we wish to determine what proportion of random faults is occurring in a large production batch. If the faults occur at random, we can get a surprisingly accurate picture by random selection of samples. We can calculate the accuracy of our estimate in relation to the number of samples we take. There is a well established technique for this in the production world, and frequently an astonishingly high level of accuracy is obtained with little effort and with very small numbers of samples.

There is a third type of statistical analysis where the selection of the samples is not random, but must be controlled. This is the type of analysis used in opinion polls. Here the number selected has little influence. The result depends on the skill with which the samples are chosen. For example, if you tried to forecast an election result by asking 2,000 left-wing supporters your result would be more inaccurate than if you only asked two people, one a left-wing supporter and one a right-wing supporter. Much foolish flourishing of large numbers (and much high expenditure) takes place in the sociological research field due to this readiness to be impressed by large numbers. In mediaeval times if you went to a doctor and he told you your insides were being devoured by seven worms you never doubted the seven (*vide* Bernard Shaw). Nowadays the general public expects millions and gets it, whether relevant or not.

In investigations of the kind described in Chapter 4 the degree of accuracy depends almost entirely on the skill with which the samples are selected, not on the number. Here we are fortunate, as motorists are much the same and face much the same conditions everywhere. Whether or not the conclusions of Chapter 4 are significant therefore depends on whether we picked normal or unusual people. We did pick a few unusual ones and there was a clear distinction between the results from these few (the specialists and the technicians) and the remainder of the samples, whose results were quite homogeneous. This is sufficient to provide near-certainty with regard to the guidance obtained.

For further information on this the reader is referred to Section 7 of the Bibliography.

APPENDIX 6

Pitfalls for the Layman

Do not be put off if some of the ideas in this book are decried by the experts. The expert must be allowed his individuality. For example, when I advocated demerit marks, I found this generally treated with contempt. Just a stunt system! Yet some of those who decried it had adopted it. They had recast it, perhaps improved it a little, and given it their own label.

It is important also not to be too impressed by erudite technical literature. Most of it, however impressive to the layman, is quite valueless. I once asked a research man in the medical world – a man of very considerable standing – what proportion of the medical literature had any value, other than in its main purpose of achieving personal advertisement. In order that he should not feel embarrassed in replying, I told him that in my profession it was about 10%. He was surprised and volunteered that it was nothing like that in the medical world – probably not as much as 5%.* In the worlds of psychology, sociology and economics the figure is undoubtedly lower again. I doubt if more than 2% of the work published has much value.

This does not mean that there is anything wrong in the set-up. No one can judge which of all the mass is the particular 2% or 5% which is of value. We have to publish it all and allow time

* Recently another leading researcher said this was ridiculous. The figure was nearer 1%, with perhaps a vestigial contribution from 5% to 10%.

and the interchange of ideas to winnow it out. All I am saying is that the layman must avoid getting caught up in this process, and not make the unjustified assumption that because a man has published a lot of articles, flourished a lot of mathematics, and generally put on a good façade, that therefore he knows what he is talking about. On the periphery of knowledge, there is no one to judge. Nothing except the test of time can decide what is the truth. Anyone who doubts this should read the technical papers of 40 years ago on any subject.

APPENDIX 7

Over-tolerant View of Killing on the Roads

Moseley (Bib. 306) emphasizes that accidents involving death are apparently by nature quite different from those involving injury. He says they are as apart as cancer and the common cold. They need a different approach and follow different factual patterns. He suggests also that quite a number of such fatal accidents are murder in the specific criminal sense – such as someone cutting nearly through a brake line, with the intention of causing the death of the driver. Willett (Bib. 302) has uncovered a criminal pattern in the serious violations (about 650) which he investigated. He finds that 'real' criminals – people involved with the police in matters other than road accidents – sometimes cause many more accidents than the average motorist. Alcohol is also much more evident in fatalities than in injuries (12.13).

When I discuss these cases I find the general reaction is 'That's quite different! Real criminals should be punished properly.'

The point that weighs most in favour of the killer on the roads is that he has no personal acquaintance with the victim, and does not set out with the intention of killing. It is a kind and human reaction, to say that he didn't really mean it. But surely the *effect* of an action must be taken into account to some degree. To hang a man, or imprison him for life when he kills with intent, and to fine him £25 when he kills without intent, makes intention the only criterion. Surely negligence and irresponsibility are not without blame. Surely the damage done must have some voice.

Just how big a discrepancy exists today is well illustrated by an account of the trial in England of seven motorists who admitted causing death by dangerous driving. They are reported in the *Daily Express* 17th December, 1964. Mr. Justice Thesiger is reported as saying: 'It must appear to the public to be an anomaly that somebody should be fined less for killing a person, than a footballer for swearing at a referee.' The punishments were regarded as of unusual severity and consisted of four months' imprisonment plus a four-year driving ban in one case, £250 fine and eight years' ban (no prison) in a second, £100 and four years' ban (no prison) in the third and the fourth; the others were apparently lighter sentences.

If one accepts the broad principle of Chapter 11 that we must get tough and make an example as far as it is possible consistent with justice, then surely those of whom an example should be made are those who kill. On the other hand, there can be no doubt that the safest and most careful motorist can on occasion be involved in an accident which results in death. Nor can there be any doubt that everyone concerned with accidents lies about them afterwards – often without realizing it. The administration of justice under these conditions is a most distressing task, and an ordeal for all concerned. So possibly the light sentences reflect a greater wisdom than is apparent at first sight.

Bibliography 606 and 607 indicate that there is considerable weight of opinion already behind the move away from 'intent'. Bib. 211 seems to indicate that some religious elements are also tending to regard negligence on the roads as a serious sin. There is no indication anywhere, as far as I can find, of any tendency to take negligence with mechanical matters more seriously, other than the fidelity scheme referred to in 10.5b. and the M.V.I. scheme of Bib. 26.

Possibly the right solution is not amenable to public discussion, as in so many of these cases. It has to be left to the discretion of the Courts, who may well on occasion judge that the ordeal of the investigation may have been an adequate lesson, and that the accused might justifiably be given the benefit of any doubt, and let off relatively lightly. But not so lightly, surely, as current views permit!

APPENDIX 8

Motivations

From the point of view of persuading people, motivations may be roughly divided into three groups:

Firstly, there is the jungle group, such as fear, need to belong, need for security, self interest, hatred, anger, jealousy, desire for pleasures such as sex, food and amusement (which can be equated frequently to money) and so on. It is interesting to observe that nearly every one of the foregoing list is pandered to by the motor-car. We cannot appeal to any of them, except fear, as a help in cutting the motor-car down to size.

Secondly, we have the egocentric group such as search for status and social prominence, self-importance, search for style, dignity and poise, the soothing of conscience or sense of guilt, and so on. All of this group too are comforted by the motor-car and are of no help to us.

Thirdly, we have the newly evolved higher group – desire for good, pity, sympathy, sense of duty and of the richness of life, and so on. These of course would be useful to us, but they are so readily inhibited by the more fundamental feelings of the first two groups that they are not very effective.

If all the powerful motivations are already stimulated in the opposite direction and work against us, what possible point of entry do we have? We have suggested social conventions, i.e. using the tribal 'need to belong'. But that produces different reactions in different social groups. If Eton and Harrow adopt a certain convention, Trafalgar Square (or some place) will guy it.

A detailed study of this would undoubtedly throw up many secondary possibilities. The fundamental framework is unlikely to be shaken. We will not find a powerful motivation. We must fall back on something factual – something we can establish in the 'knowery'. People 'know' that fire burns. They don't have to have emotions to make them careful of it. This is the great attraction of the vulnerability conception, or of Malfetti's electronic alarm.

APPENDIX 9

Teaching Morality

If a young person finds an accepted behaviour code in his surroundings; if there is firm discipline in enforcing this code, with punishment for departure and approbation for conformity; if there is around him an imperative command to conform; if the community takes it for granted that anyone who 'belongs' will conform; then nearly all young people accept this code blindly, without challenge, no matter what it is. In any such integrated community different sections provide the different reactions needed by the young. They go to one group of people for friendship and sympathy; another group exercises discipline; another group applies some kind of persuasive education; and there is always a group exercising a certain amount of intimidation, whom the young view with some awe. If these groups are nicely balanced and support each other, then growth and the civilizing process take place quite painlessly. If the sympathy is overdone, so that it is interpreted as failure to support the discipline; if the discipline is too harsh and obviously unfair; if the intimidatory elements are clearly not working for general welfare but for selfish interests; then the young discern this and fail to respond. This is what is happening today, with the addition of very strong movements aiming actually to corrupt the young. This latter activity was once punishable under the criminal code, but is now a big and successful industry.

There are in any era many such codes, covering religion, morals, ethics, manners, clothes, social conventions, and so on. The firmer and more clear-cut the code, the more conspicuous is anyone who breaks it. Those who long to stand out from the general mass and attract personal attention have always used this fact. The shocking work of art, the exaggerated dress, the parade of degeneracy, the sneer technique, and so on – they are all familiar and bring great rewards to those that have the stomach to go to the necessary lengths. Today it is in particular the denigration of morality which is so exploited by those seeking the limelight. It has seriously corrupted our young, many of whom are completely fooled by it, and begin to admire sneer techniques as some kind of superior intellectual activity.

Under these circumstances it becomes largely true that morality cannot be taught.

Here we have a problem covering a much wider area than just road accidents. Perhaps it is as well to remember that the German hausfrau welcomed Hitler (I was working there and heard it again and again) chiefly because he cleaned up the pornographic magazines and similar degenerate activities, and brought the German youth back with a jerk to moral behaviour and a sense of social duty. The youth loved it and felt restored to health after a long sickness. Perhaps we ought to get started ourselves, before another Hitler gets in ahead of us.

APPENDIX 10

Automatic Mental Processes

We have said that learning to handle a car is from some aspects rather like learning to play a game, such as squash or tennis. 'Learning' in this case consists of a constant correction and re-establishment of the computer sequences required to give the muscular co-ordinations called up by the will. This has to be a completely automatic process. There can be no two-stage mental process involved – as soon get out the book to look up how to handle a fast serve when you see it coming. After sufficient practice the mind is so conditioned that one simple message from the will – willing the ball to go into a certain position, or the car to follow a certain pattern – is all that is needed. In response to this one simple effort tens of thousands of signals pour out from the computer part of the mind, all of precisely the right intensity and with the right time sequence, to produce the complex interplay of muscular reactions which are required. Some of these sequences come from the brain, others from nervous sub-centres, much in the same way as certain standard formulae are kept set up in sub-centres of a computer.

Practice in this case is largely a mental process. I have read of an experiment in which twenty tennis players were made to practice a good many hours a day every day for three weeks. Another group of twenty were made to practice in the same way, but only in their imagination. For the whole three weeks they were not allowed to touch a racket or a ball. It was claimed that at the end of the three weeks the improvement in the two groups was indistinguishable. I have used this myself in teaching squash. I always advise the pupil to practice in his imagination in bed before he goes to sleep. The improvement which results is sometimes fantastic.

It is extremely easy to interfere in this miraculous and awe-inspiring mechanism. If a two-stage conscious process is allowed to become a habit, the acquisition of the one-stage automatic functioning is much delayed, if not inhibited. To take a simple example, if one is taught the morse code by learning that dot dash equals A this makes it much harder for the mind to learn that a certain sound (da-daa) equals A. This is because there has been created a tendency to turn da-daa into dot-dash and thence into A. This two-stage process demands conscious thinking. The one stage speedily becomes automatic.

Much teaching of foreign languages makes the same error. The automatic way to speak is to say what you want to with the words you have. If the habit of translating intervenes it is always a labour, and ease in any language is unattainable.

To take an example nearer home, the plugging of minimum stopping distances (see 9.4), although so valuable in waking a motorist up to the dangers of getting too close, could do harm if it induced a process of stopping involving two-stage thinking. The reason why the reader probably did not know the stopping distances is that he does not need to know. He uses the one-stage process – an acquired skill in his mind. It goes like this – 'There is an obstacle. Can I stop before I reach it?' Nothing whatever comes in between – all estimates of speed and distance are quite automatic. Imagine how dangerous it would be if instead the mind had to say 'There is an obstacle. How many yards away is it? What is my speed? Can I stop at that speed in that number of yards?'

There is much need in the modern outlook to rediscover the limitations of teaching. One cannot teach how to be a great man, or a successful artist, or how to write a play. One cannot teach artistic appreciation, or musical appreciation, or how to handle people, or any of a thousand other higher tasks which we are capable of mastering. One can only block the faculty from ever flowering. There is a fundamental reason for this – the powers of achievement will always go beyond the power of analysis. Teaching can only be useful where the achievement can be analysed and some generalizations deduced from the analysis.

Some *elements* of analysis are perhaps possible. Something is learned from listening to a great achiever telling you how he does it.* Something is learned from a correspondence course on how to write novels. But what is learned is only a small part. Too much emphasis on learning and too much listening to imperfect rules will prevent the realization of full powers of achievement. This basic error of thinking reaches its heights when one hears politicians talking about setting up training classes in diplomacy, and universities establishing chairs in business management. These form a useful basis. No one suggests that they are of no value. But they do not guide the whole way – they only give a point of entry and a couple of signposts at the start of a journey into a country that must be wild and unknown to every traveller and which must be entered by every traveller on his own, in his own way, and at his own speed.

* Though mostly he doesn't know. What he thinks he does is often quite different from what he actually does.

APPENDIX 11

Insoluble Administration Problems of the Police

The point has been made in Section 11.7 that the police are faced with many illogicalities and contradictions which cannot be reconciled. Whatever policy is adopted to solve this situation is likely to be ineffective if it is publicized. Leave it to the authorities, it was suggested, and support them blindly.

As this leaves the reader rather in mid-air, I now give here one solution to this predicament for an area where speed limits cannot be enforced. This is given solely to round off the picture, not under any delusions that in reality such a difficult problem could be disposed of so easily.

The police would accept all the illogicalities and contradictions of the speed limit situation and make no attempt to put them right. It is quite possible for the public to accept a situation full of illogicalities without discerning it. Every possible violation would be booked and fined. There would be no warnings if a provable violation had occurred. The force would be briefed to explain that in these matters there was no discretion. It was the law and the police had to enforce it. Motorists must obey the law precisely. There would be no borderline cases allowed to get away. A respect for, and even apologetic attitude to, offenders would be inculcated, and much time devoted to training patrols in the propaganda aspects of the job and in the details of public relationship. On parting the officer would make it a rule to say 'we have to cut down the injuries, sir.'

The number of patrols would be stepped up to obtain an average of one booking per year per motorist. This would mean that bad motorists would be shown up clearly within two or three years.

Patrols would be briefed that in the areas and at the times where speed limits cannot be enforced they must not be there. They must never turn a blind eye.

Much money would be spent on inducing a feeling of police omnipresence.

The basic objective would be that every person penalized should approve of the penalty. There would be a demerit mark system with five marks calling down a three-months' licence suspension. Three months is plenty to achieve the effect sought on the wicked ones, and not too desperately heavy on the unlucky ones.

Much effort would be devoted to making sure that the man about to incur the licence disqualification saw it coming before he let it hit him. For example, there would be a corps of the most understanding, patient and impressive officers that could be found, with the job of selling the idea to people whose demerit marks were beginning to mount up. These offenders would be invited to visit headquarters and this special corps would devote much time to discussing the whole problem with them. They would be advised to avoid anger when they see other people driving badly. They would be told about counting vulnerabilities. In time, an effective technique would undoubtedly develop. This special corps need not be large. It would be made up of men of top standing, able to establish an ascendancy of personality over all comers. Top salaries would be essential.

A proportion of conversations would be recorded and studied afterwards by a separate supervisory group, which might include a few specialists such as public relations experts and psychologists.

The last thing permitted in these discussions would be any appearance of toughness. People are not antagonized by what is done to them, but by the way it is done. The objective would be to send each man away, convinced that he was getting a very favourable deal from the police, and that if he did not improve his driving they would be quite right in punishing him severely. This way he would be thinking so hard about himself that he would not be too preoccupied with the fact that there were other drivers just as bad who hadn't been caught. He might even become an advocate for catching them too! i.e., if we handle him skilfully he might ultimately come over to our side.

The patrols would be encouraged to pull up every case where there was inconsiderate driving, not an actual violation, and to use the 'courtesy cop' line – a very friendly, respectful warning. This would help quite a lot in the 'untough' image creation (which has to be in the mind of the patrols as well as the public).

As soon as it was felt that the omnipresence feeling was sufficiently established, it would be possible to raise some speed limits, de-control certain roads, and begin to reduce the gap between legislation and enforcement.

You see how completely all this would be defeated if ever the policy were admitted to anyone, even officers of the force. What would be publicized would be something quite different – something which made much of police reasonableness and *untoughness* in a field which didn't matter too much. Any reference to the masses of violations which were perforce being ignored would be played down and side-stepped. No attempt to justify it would be made. Nothing would be said by the police, and they would fail to hear anything anyone else said.

The roads job would be seen as quite distinct from police work, as generally understood, and would use a new series of terms. There would be a separate traffic force, with a separate uniform, for the roads. This force would be briefed that their main function would be simply that of creating a certain mood in the mind of the public. Every possible public relations device would be incorporated into this.

Within a year the initial outcry would die down, and within two years the public would have got used to the idea that there were no margins and no border-line cases. After five years, they would begin to be proud of the local tradition, and of the excellent accident figures which would undoubtedly show up.

Road safety is completely different from any other law enforcement task. The problem is uniquely difficult, and will only be solved by those who have the courage to break with the orthodox and accept a much greater level of personal responsibility than is usual. It is all a little like Stalky's headmaster, who, if you remember, called him in after he had completely outwitted one of the other masters and explained that he had fully recognized Stalky's position was unassailable; Stalky had done nothing wrong, and no punishment could possibly be justified. Nevertheless, he was going to flog him. And he did! Stalky approved.

APPENDIX 12

Draft Letter from Police to Offender

Dear Sir,

I have been assigned by the Chief Commissioner of Police to obtain co-operation from the Public in his task of reducing road accidents.

I see that you were booked recently in an infringement of the road regulations. You probably felt that this was rather a secondary matter, which happens to everyone, but for which not everyone is booked. You may not be aware of the role that these minor infringements play in traffic accidents. When you see a wild driver cutting in or passing on the wrong side, exceeding the speed limit and disappearing from sight, you may tend to say 'There's the man the police should catch. He's the one that produces the accidents, not me.' All the recent investigations on traffic accidents contradict this view. Most accidents are not caused by the wild activities of a few, but by the occasional lapses of the ordinary careful driver. Most motorists take such momentary risks only a few times a week. In effect they go 'wild' for a moment. The true wild man may commit a thousand such lapses in a week. But there are a thousand careful motorists for one wild man. (You may not readily accept this because you notice the wild man more, but the facts are beyond dispute.) Four or five momentary wildnesses a week by a thousand ordinary people add up to much more than 1,000 from one bad man.

Therefore, your minor infringement is very important to us. From the point of view of your own safety, it is also important to you. Risks cannot be divided into ones that matter and ones that don't. There is no knowing what a minor lapse may precipitate. The total number of accidents is determined by the total number of these risks; it is only by reducing the total number of these very unimportant things that we can secure this very important effect.

This means that the task of the Chief Commissioner is to persuade the ordinary motorist to cut out all lapses from a high standard of safety. This is why we are obliged to treat all infringements seriously, and to bring increasing pressure to bear on those who by a sequence of bookings, show that they are more dangerous than the average.

It is a little difficult to say to a man who does nothing very dangerous that he is still the main danger. Yet this is the truth. The average man goes 30 years without a crash. Yet the 10,000 little dangers that he produces in those 30 years are, in total, the main cause of accidents.

This being clearly established, the Chief Commissioner has no choice but to remove from the roads those who contribute too much to the main danger. Fortunately this can be done with great fairness, by keeping a record of bookings. One odd carelessness may well be a matter of chance, which the Chief Commissioner has no desire to penalize unduly. It is a sequence that brands a motorist and which must be acted on by withdrawal of licence. The procedure which is followed is this:

Loss of licence may follow the accumulation of eight points in two years or twelve in three years. Scale of points:*

Three points: Speeding; reckless driving.
Two points: Ignoring traffic signals; Inadequate brakes; Following too closely, etc.
One point: Failure to signal properly; Illegal turn, etc.

The concentrated dangers produced by the really wild driver are, of course, still important and very much in the mind of the Chief Commissioner. These are followed up whenever detected, and there is no hesitation to ask for heavy penalties from the start. Such cases can never be completely eliminated from the roads, however, if only because many of them are derived from newcomers – drivers in the first excitement of a new car, or young people in the first flush of manhood. When

---

*Extracted, in a very incomplete form, from New York State Drivers Manual, 1961. Quoted only to convey general idea.

you see such cases, often flagrant ones, as you always will, do not blame the police too much, and even more important, do not let it invade your own peace of mind, and make you angry. An angry driver is always more vulnerable, so that you do yourself no service.

I would be happy to discuss this with you and show you the evidence for the above statements, if you are interested. A small discussion group meets from time to time and we should much appreciate your help in this work. There is much that you can do. Please contact ——

Yours etc.

A similar letter to this could also be sent to those who have just had an accident.

APPENDIX 13

Estimate of Unbooked Violations and Proportion of Wild Drivers

Assume (Approximately U.K. conditions)
  7 million cars
  1 million bookings per annum
  2 patrol-hours on the road per booking
  2 million patrol-hours per annum
  Average time for which vehicle is under supervision – 10 secs.
  Average supervision per patrol – 1,000 vehicles per hour $\equiv$ 1,000 10-sec. intervals

  Average motorist averages 1 hour per day and V violations per annum $\equiv$ approximately 100,000 10-sec. intervals per annum. Average number of bookings 1 in 7 years.

Amount of Supervision
  7 million motorists $\equiv 7 \times 10^6 \times 10^5$ intervals, each 10 sec.
  2 million patrol-hours $\equiv 2 \times 10^6 \times 10^3$ intervals supervised.
  $\therefore$ motorist is under supervision:

$$\frac{1 \text{ in } 7 \times 10^{11}}{2 \times 10^9} = 1 \text{ in } 350$$

Probabilities for One Motorist

During any one particular interval the chances he violates are

$$\frac{V}{10^5}$$

The chances that he is seen are $\dfrac{V}{10^5} \times \dfrac{1}{350}$

Therefore over 7 years each of 10^5 intervals the chances he is seen are:

$$\frac{V}{10^5} \times \frac{1}{350} \times 7 \times 10^5 = \frac{V}{50}$$

As the average is once in 7 years V = 50.

Proportion of Wild Drivers

From above, 2,000 vehicles are supervised per booking. If four bookings out of five are for minor offences, and the fifth a wild driver, then the proportion of wild drivers is 1 in 2,000 × 5 = 0·01%.

Allowing a factor of 10:1 for cunning in spotting the police it is still only 0.1%. The figure of 1 in 5 for wild drivers is very much on the safe side. For example, in N.S.W. only one booking in fifty is for a serious offence involving automatic disqualification.

This says nothing about whether the wild drivers are habitual or occasional. Certainly not all will be habitual.

Proportion of Drivers Who are Habitually Wild (BBTN2a)

Some indication of this should be deducible from records of repeated citations. Unfortunately I have been unable to find any work on what proportion of multiple citations would be the result of chance. My own rather uncertain efforts indicate that the position is vastly different in different communities.

In one case warnings were apparently issued after three citations over a two-year period to 1.1% of drivers and disqualification was subsequently applied to 0.2%. In this case my attempt at calculating the probabilities indicated that for 3X-citations eight out of ten would be the result of random distribution and only two genuine habitual bad drivers. For 4X-citations probably only two out of ten would be victims of chance and the other eight would be deservedly penalized. This seems to line up almost too well with the proportion of 3X-citations ultimately disqualified, and indicates one habitual high-rate violator per five hundred drivers. I cite this case with diffidence as I had difficulty in getting adequate data, and am by no means sure of my mathematics.

There is here an interesting and challenging opportunity for research, because the results would help us to apply the more severe penalizations with greater certainty of fairness.

APPENDIX 14

Prejudice against Demerit Marks

Demerit marking systems are widely disliked because of the connotations of a dossier. For example, the French Chamber rejected a police recommendation for such a scheme by an over-whelming vote (84%) probably from memories of wartime abuses.

Some readers may fail to realize just how dossiers deliver their subjects into the hands of the public servant or the subversive group. Every entry gives an opportunity to put a slant to the picture. Unjust or slightly false items can be added to prejudice anyone who calls up the dossier, and the victim can never discover what is against him, or give an answer to it. The dossier represents the nadir of justice, and bureaucracy at its worst.

However, the same objections apply to any police documents, and are not really any special objection to the demerit marking system. Any judgement-on-the-spot system puts the patrol man's version on the record, and there is no come-back. The police must obviously be free to record even remote suspicions and refuse all access to their files. For this reason, objections to demerit marking systems are largely prejudice. The system can be made as free of abuses as any other by writing into the law a clause that anyone receiving a demerit mark should be advised of it, with details as to when it was incurred and why.

He should have the right of appeal to the Court if he wants to use it. Probably the right of appeal should not lapse until the demerit mark itself lapses.

Possibly some of the pet theories for creating dossiers by means of reports from amateur police (12.2) have helped discredit the system.

The system has been introduced in England without running into these troubles by two simple steps: firstly, making licence endorsement obligatory for any major violation; and secondly, making three endorsements produce automatic withdrawal of licence (see Road Traffic Act 1962). The licence is then the only dossier – an admirable set-up, one would think.

APPENDIX 15

Examples of Vulnerabilities

Here are a few examples of vulnerabilities that are fairly common. As suggested in 9.8, it is not important if the suggested tactics are not acceptable. Procedures differ greatly in different communities.

(1) Overtaking without sufficient margins. This may occur due to misjudgement of the distance to an approaching corner, or to misjudgement of speed of an approaching vehicle. If this vulnerability is observed frequently it is a good idea to carry out a few experiments. Get a friend to drive towards you at different speeds and try to estimate the speeds, firstly when you are stationary and secondly when you drive towards him. Some people can do this with uncanny accuracy, and some people make astonishing errors. Rospa House (Bib. 205) have a machine to test the ability to discern relative positions of two vehicles.

(2) The car ahead pulls out while you are overtaking, because of an obstacle you did nōt see.

(3) The car ahead pulls out because he decides to overtake just as you do.

(4) As you begin to overtake, the car ahead speeds up, and either destroys your margins, or closes up a gap into which you plan to move. This is sometimes a matter of un-civilized behaviour on the part of the other driver, in which case it is important that you should not get angry. You have no hope of arriving at maturity unless you accept the fact that others are perhaps not so far along the path as yourself. It is as well to remember, however, that there may be other legitimate reasons why he speeded up. Perhaps he was going to speed up, anyway, and hadn't seen that you were over-taking. Perhaps your own method of passing had inconsider-ate aspects. You may have irritated him by hooting in an unskilled way or an offensive way. Perhaps you were taking such a chance that he became angry and was trying to teach you a lesson. He shouldn't do this, of course, but you, your-self, in that case contributed.

(5) Inadequate Allowance for a Side Entry.

If you are not at all times able to avoid an unforeseen entry from the side you are vulnerable. The important thing to do in this situation is not only to watch speed but also make sure that the foot is off the accelerator and poised over the brake. This will halve the free run (see App. 1). If under this condition you are doing 30 m.p.h. with your foot on the accelerator you will sail along for about 33 feet. before the brake is applied at all. By holding the foot over the brake pedal you can cut this to 16 feet.

(6) Driving too close to parked cars. You cannot rely on being able to see that there is no one in every car. If you try to, you will distract yourself from other hazards. Therefore you must leave enough space for a door to be opened slightly as you pass. This can be taken too far, as the times involved are not such that anyone could open the door the whole way and jump out. Three feet of clearance at ordinary speeds is quite safe, but one foot is absolutely murderous. In the latter case, every car you pass should be counted as a separate vulnerability.

(7) Failure to observe that another car is about to pull out in front of you. The fact that you have the right of way

and it is a particularly foolish thing for him to do, is quite irrelevant.

(8) Following too closely behind another vehicle while awaiting an opportunity to pass. If one stays at a safe distance this is interpreted by those behind as meaning that one does not wish to pass. They then sometimes force past and cut in. This is particularly infuriating, but has to be accepted.

Here are a few examples of more obscure vulnerabilities:

(*a*) Failure to brake hard when visibility lost. If you are blinded by an oncoming headlight, or if you run into a sudden patch of fog, or if for any other reason you cannot see the road ahead for a greater distance than your stopping powers, then you must always assume that there is something like a cow or a child on the road dead ahead of you and brake as hard as you dare. Many drivers fail to observe this precaution because of the fear of having another driver on their tail.

(*b*) Allowing the car behind to stay at an unsafe closeness while at speed. This means that any sudden braking will cause a collision from behind as well as what may happen in front. The only possible move here – and, unfortunately, very few people do this – is to slow down gradually until the distance between you and the tailing car is safe. Sometimes this means dropping right back to 20 m.p.h. or less. If you don't do this you are vulnerable every moment you drive, and you should probably count vulnerabilities on a fairly pessimistic basis. If you want to work it out accurately (which is never necessary) I suppose you should count a vulnerability for every car you pass, and for every side entry, pedestrian, cyclist, etc. It is desperate unwisdom to stay in such a vulnerable position.

This is a situation which emphasizes the unwisdom of relying on signals. Current teaching techniques in many places place far too much emphasis on signals. The signal can never be given in a real emergency. There simply isn't time. Insistence on hand signals diminishes the significance of the stop signal given automatically with the application of the brake. Motorists should be taught to rely entirely on this signal and to see it as of much greater significance than any hand signal. An extremely valuable device which could be developed with much ease would be a two-stage automatic signal – a normal red light for a normal application of the brake and a very large and obtrusive signal which should appear when a violent application of the brake takes place.

(*c*) Remaining in a position of danger when someone is overtaking. If someone overtakes unwisely and you see a possibility of an accident, clearly you are vulnerable. It may not be your fault. But you must certainly count it as a vulnerability unless you have done your utmost to wriggle out of the position irrespective of whose fault it is. Immediate braking is called for.

(*d*) Inadequate allowance for a possible wobble by a cyclist. It is no excuse if an oncoming car leaves you inadequate room for this. In such a case you must brake violently. This applies also to a pedestrian on the side of the road.

(*e*) Driving so close to the kerb that one step of a pedestrian just off the edge would be enough to produce a hit. With normal speeds of movement possibly a foot is enough to safeguard against this, and very few motorists in most countries fail to observe this amount of margin. In my own personal experience the outstanding exception is in England, where there seems a nearly insane desire to show how accurately one can place the car by driving as near to the kerb as possible. I found this one of the strangest and most perturbing aspects of motoring in England, and quite beyond comprehension. It must surely be responsible for many accidents.

(*f*) Failing to brake hard and take other evasive action when a crash seems to be forming up ahead. Very few people are able to visualize what will happen, until they see some car out of control hurtling towards them.

(*g*) Failing to study the possible trajectory of an oncoming car going out of control round a corner. One should deliberately dodge – speed up or slow down or pull off the road, so as to get out of the line of fire.

The foregoing list is, of course, in no way complete. Nor, for reasons given in 9.8 could much be gained by attempting to complete it.

APPENDIX 16

The Persecution Process

There is a very simple process in Society whereby prejudices get associated with certain labels. If a man treats you badly, you may tend to curse him. But if you notice that he bears a label it is not a very difficult process to extend your curses to cover the label. For example, instead of saying, that confounded driver! you say, that confounded woman driver! or that confounded youth driver! This spreading of the prejudice from the individual to the group is quite fearsome in the rapidity with which it operates and the violence which it engenders. Every individual imperfection of every member of the group gets blamed on to the group, and in no time at all, everyone is hopelessly prejudiced. Women drivers, like Jews, have suffered under this for a long time. We now see it extending rapidly to youths, drunks, drivers of powerful cars, old people and drivers of old cars. When these categories are involved in an accident they don't stand a chance. Automatically, the police or any other investigators tick the appropriate column as the cause of the accident, and impartial inquiry simply doesn't happen.

If you hear of a dithering and senile old lady stepping into the road right under the wheel of the car, you tend to be sorry for the driver as well as for the old lady. But if you hear it was a youth driving a sports car do you feel the same? Or do you, in spite of all attempts to be fair, feel nearly sure it was his fault? Most of us do.

The worst effect of this is not its injustice, even, but the nervousness and uncertainty it creates in anybody carrying the label. Where the complex skills of driving are involved anxiety is a fearsome inhibitor and a great cause of danger. We are today persecuting our youth, our drinkers, our women drivers and several other hysterically labelled groups, in the real old-fashioned sense of the word. There is much evidence that great harm is being done, in the form of actually increasing the accidents. Still a third effect is produced – public attention is directed away from the real causes of the trouble. The outcry for more stringent driving tests, provisional driving licences and quick cancellation of them, and the like, is often overworked and is sometimes aggravating the situation.

APPENDIX 17

Discourtesy as an Indictable Offence

Another aspect of the ethics/law conflict arises from discourtesy on the roads. If a bully bluffs you off the sidewalk you are wise to ignore it. A bystanding policeman is also probably wise to turn a blind eye. But discourtesy on the roads frequently leads to further troubles – often very bad ones. Can we afford to ignore it?

There is much to be said for making discourtesy itself an indictable offence. As part of a demerit mark system, with relatively mild penalization, this would surely not be too difficult to administer, once there were an adequate system of patrols.

There is a wide range of practices indulged in by some motorists which contribute to the feeling of danger and uncertainty on the roads without being indictable. Such practices are cutting in, driving too close, maintaining speed until the last moment and then braking hard, hooting as a protest, headlight flashing – the list is endless. A caution or a courteous police discussion – so much advocated – is not by any means always effective. Police officers will tell their superiors how successful cautions are, because any other line implies that they are not skilled in dealing with the public. But off the record they will tell of endless truculences and much humiliation. 'Are you going to book me or not, copper? If not, shut your trap', says the tough, convinced that the warning is being used only because the evidence is insufficient for anything stronger.

Bibliography

General Studies

1. D.S.I.R. Road Research Laboratory.
   Research on Road Safety.
   H.M. Stationery Office, Kingsway, London, W.C.2. 42s.
   602 pages.
   Comprehensive review of the accident situation.
   The British Road Research Laboratory spends about
   £1½ million per annum. Contains excellent biblio-
   graphies on all aspects. The section on The Driver
   (page 139) includes the following:
   - (9) Cobb Lauer de Silva, etc. Automobile driver
     tests administered to 3,663 persons in Connecti-
     cut 1936 to 1937, and the relation of test scores
     to the accidents sustained. Highway Research
     Board Report, Washington, D.C., 1939 (un-
     published).
   - (22) U.S.A. Government. Accidents/Driver decrease
     with age. House document No. 462 Motor
     Vehicle traffic conditions in U.S.A. Part 6.
     The accident-prone driver. Washington, D.C.
     1938 (U.S. Government Printing Office) page 36.
   - (23) Lauer. Age and sex in relation to accidents.
     Bulletin Highway Research Board, 1952 (60).
     25–35.
   - (32) Tillman and Hobbs. The accident-prone auto-
     mobile driver: a study of psychiatric and social
     background. American Journal of Psychiatry,
     1949. 106 (5) 321—31.

2. *Hazards of the Road.*
   Proceedings of Third Annual Scientific Meeting, 1962.
   British Academy of Forensic Sciences.
   The Law Society, Chancery Lane, London, W.C.2.

A series of articles covering many aspects. Those relevant to the present study are entered as separate items in this bibliography. (116/9)

3. Smeed.
   Methods available to reduce the number of road casualties.
   Summarized in Traffic Engineering and Control, December 1964, pages 509 and 523.
   Full text in O.T.A. *International Road Safety and Traffic Review* 1964. 12 (4) (Autumn Issue).
   Gives measures over the whole range of usages, which could be expected to produce reductions in casualties in England. In each case a convincing basis for the calculation is given, but the author emphasizes that he does not necessarily advocate the changes. See 10.1 for more details. The only doubtful point is whether enough allowance has been made for the step-up in risk-taking which follows any improvement in facilities, unless awareness can be lifted at the same time by some such technique as observing vulnerabilities (e.g. 10.7 Seat belts). (116/56)

4. *List of Publications*. The Traffic Institute. Hinman Avenue, Evanston, Illinois.
   'From the Institute's original goal – to provide law enforcement officers with a scientific understanding of street and highway systems – a broad educational and developmental program has evolved.' The Institute produces a large number of publications, mainly directed towards police and other public officials. See also 101, 102. (100/4, 116/47, 116/73)

5. Vernon.
   Accidents and their Prevention.
   Cambridge University Press, 1936. (116/107)

6. Statement by the Australian Automobile Association to the Senate Select Committee on Road Safety, dated 1st

April, 1960. See Report No. S2 (Group F and H)
F.7352/60, Mitchell Library reference N̲Q̲.̲ ̲6̲1̲4̲,̲ ̲8̲6̲2̲.

1

A lucid and comprehensive survey of the situation at
that time. (B.B.T. A2a)

7. National Safety Council, 425 North Michigan Avenue,
   Chicago, Ill. 60611, produces a wide range of information.

8. Norman.
   Road Traffic Accidents – Epidemiology Control and Prevention.
   World Health Organization, Geneva.
   Public Health Papers No. 12. Mitchell Library Ref:
   N̲6̲1̲4̲.̲0̲6̲.̲
   46
   Interesting summary on page 104 of Research that is
   needed.

9. *Traffic in Towns.* The Buchanan Report.
   H.M. Stationery Office, Kingsway, London, W.C.2.
   £2 10s.
   This includes some vividly presented accident data,
   notably diagrams page 18. 73% of accidents take place in
   U.K. in urban areas, but there is a higher proportion of
   deaths on the open road (as in most countries). (116/31)

10. Directory of Traffic Safety Organizations.
    National Safety Council, 425, North Michigan Avenue,
    Chicago, Ill. 60611.

11. *Recommendations on Road Safety.*
    R.A.C., Pall Mall, London, S.W.1. Pamphlet 12 pages,
    March 1964.
    Quotes, and largely endorses, London Commissioner
    of Police, 'the presence of uniformed policemen, clearly
    recognizable as such, is the finest deterrent to incon-
    siderate driving, the basic cause of all accidents'. Gives

summary of results of the 1938 Lancashire experiment in 'courtesy cops', resulting in a reduction of casualties (43%) but less in deaths (18%). Recommends (1) more police patrols, operating 'by advice, example and admonition'. (2) Review speed limits till reasonable, and then enforce. (116/48)

12. *Electronic Controls and Traffic Safety.*
Editor James L. Malfetti.
Safety Research etc. Project. Teachers College, Columbia University, N.Y., 1958. 94 pages.
Group of articles for conference with final report (116/53). Includes basic analyses on what is desirable, of great value to any commercial organization thinking of entering the field. There would appear to be considerable prospects for a proximity alarm.

13. Chafetz.
Liquor the Servant of Man.
Little, Nunn. 236 pages. $4.95.
Dr. Chafetz, director of the Alcohol Clinic at Massachusetts General Hospital puts some perspective into the subject. The cause of many accidents may not be the drinking, but the mental distress that led to the drinking. Enforcement authorities may well be too hasty to equate drinking with crime. Reviewed *Time*. South Pacific Edition, 28th May 1956.

14. *Electronic Alarms.*
A 'Driv-a-Test' electronic unit is marketed by Hub Motor Sales, 2105 W. Genesee Street, Syracuse, N.Y. It actuates an alarm when steering wheel corrections show signs of flagging.
An electronic eye steering system was described in the *New York Motorist*, May 1965, with an alarm to call in the driver, and then put on the brakes.
Information by courtesy of Doctor Malfetti, (NEI.M.).

15. *Accidents on Main Rural Highways related to Speed, Driver, Vehicle.*
U.S. Govt. Printing Office, Washington, D.C. 30412. Bureau of Public Roads Study analysing the accident records of nearly 10,000 drivers, plus speed observations and interviews with 290,000 drivers. Covered 10 States. Accident rate is lowest at the natural speed of the highway – see Fig. 9, p.16. Slowness appears to be as fruitful as speed (cf. 10.1 on British prejudice). Severity of accident follows a different pattern – increasing with speed. Fatality rate was lowest at average speed. Fig. 12, p.26, shows clearly that involvement rate is greater with lower horse power. (cf. 12.10 on high powered cars). Female drivers over 35 years old, contrary to general impression, consistently had higher accident-involvement rates than male drivers.

This study demolishes so many pet theories that it is perhaps the first choice of all in recommended reading. For example: 'Drivers 40 years of age travelling at 65 m.p.h. in cars 2 years old with 200 h.p. averaged one reported accident in 1,600,000 miles of driving. In contrast drivers 18 years old travelling at 30 m.p.h. in cars 6 years old with 100 h.p. averaged one reported accident in 12,000 miles'. (116/9H)

16. *Accident Research: Methods and Approaches.*
Haddon, Suchman, and Klein, Harper & Row, New York and London. 752 pages.

17. de Silva.
Why We Have Automobile Accidents. Wiley. 1942. 60/-.

18. Halsey, Ed.
Accident Prevention. McGraw Hill. 93/-.

19. Barmack.
Methodological Problems in the Design of Motor Vehicle Accident Research. American Journal of Public Health, Vol. 52, No. 11, November 1962. (116/84).

20. Haddon.
    A Note Concerning Accident Theory and Research with Special Reference to Motor Vehicle Accidents.
    Annals of the New York Academy of Sciences, Vol. 107, Article 2, pages 635-646. May 22, 1963. (116/87).

21.
    Research Grants in Accident Prevention to July 1964.
    Division of Accident Prevention, Public Health Service, U.S. Dept. of Health, Washington 25, D.C.
    Lists 93 research projects, each involving very substantial expenditure, sponsored by the Division of Accident Prevention. Addresses from which information about these specific projects can be obtained are included. (116/62)

22. Whitelaw.
    Bibliography of Highway Traffic Safety with Annotations. 1956–1960.
    Reprinted by U.S. Dept. of Health, Division of Accident Prevention, Washington, D.C. 110 pp. 1961.
    Mr. Whitelaw is Librarian of the Highway Traffic Safety Centre, Michigan State University, East Lansing, Mich. (116/59)

23. McFarland and Associates
    Publications in the Field of Highway Safety 1951–1961.
    Accident Research Programme, Harvard School of Health. Boston, Mass. 14 pages.
    A very valuable short list. A supplementary sheet covering recent additions to the above has also been issued.

24. *Organising a Citizens' Traffic Safety Council.*
    New York State Traffic Council, 23 E. 26th Street, N.Y. 10010. 1962. 14 pages.
    Suggestions on how to start a voluntary road safety council. (116/95)

25. McCarroll and Haddon.
    A Controlled Study of Fatal Automobile Accidents in New York City.
    Dept. of Public Health, Cornell University Medical College, New York and the Epidemiology Residency Program New York State Dept. of Health, Albany. 1961. (116/89)
    Journal Chron. Dis. 15 811. Pergamon Press.

26. *Motor Vehicle Inspection Reference Guide.*
    American Association of Motor Vehicle Administration, 404 Madison Building, Washington, D.C., 20005.
    Much general data assembled in effective style. Mentions a test in Wichita in which out of 36,281 vehicles checked, 42% had one or more unsafe tyres; and the Kentucky State Fair check in 1963, when 2,500 fairgoers' vehicles were 73% mechanically unfit due to maintenance neglect. The M.V.I. programme, which is voluntary, has checked 30m. vehicles over the period 1954–1964 and found 4.5m. with one or more safety hazards. Cites Swedish case: In 152 one-car accidents 27% ascribed to faulty vehicles. Part 1., pages 19–22, gives details of M.V.I. programmes by State. (116/9H)

27. *Proposal for the Creation of an International Safety Organisation.*
    The American Museum of Safety, 85 John Street, New York, N.Y. 10038. 18 pages. 1964.
    Also supplementary brochure, 18 pages, expanding the suggestions.
    Covers a proposal for an international body to handle all aspects of safety, not limited to road accidents. Lists existing international organisations. (116/67)

28. *The Action Programme.*
    The President's Committee for Traffic Safety, 532 Pennsylvania Building, Washington, 4, D.C. 38 pages. 1962.

Gives long list of recommendations on all aspects, but little indication of relative importance or effectiveness. There are separate supplementary booklets on different aspects, all obtainable from the U.S. Government Printing Office, Washington 25, D.C. (116/80)

29. *Annual Report 1964.*
   Insurance Institute for Highway Safety, 1725 De Sales Street, N.W., Washington, D.C. 20036.
   This Institute devotes large sums to the financial support of various safety organizations. Its budget for 1964 was $1,690,000 of which 87% was contributed to such organizations. This report gives an interesting picture of the over-all structure of safety work in U.S.A. (116/68)

30. Williams.
   The Nonsense about Safe Driving.
   Fortune, September 1958, pages 118/9.
   The author is head of the Mathematics Division of Rand Corporations; endeavours to bring some perspective into the approach. A useful antidote to some of the hysteria becoming evident in administrative circles, and some stimulating new suggestions such as a plea for more advanced signalling equipment on vehicles.
   The flashing of all four turning lights to indicate disablement (soon to be compulsory in N.Y.) is a good example of this. (116/131)

31. Paterson.
   Report: *Overseas Survey Road Safety Practices.*
   Australian Road Safety Council. 1959. (116/91)

32. *Driving is an Art.*
   National Roads and Motorists Associations (N.S.W.) Booklet. 24 pages.

33. Patterson.
   Road Safety.

Special issue of *Current Affairs Bulletin* (vol. 12, No. 13). Published by Tutorial Classes Department, University of Sydney. Reprints available from Australian Road Safety Council, Melbourne. 28 pages. 1964.
Valuable summary of the position, with vivid presentation of statistics. (116/58)

34. Australian Road Safety Council, 497 Collins Street, Melbourne, produces a wide range of posters, leaflets, and data for publicity drives. Also teaching textbook (219) and kits for public speakers. Wide range of films available.

35. *The Reasons for Periodic Motor Vehicle Inspection.*
Automotive Service Industry Association, 168 North Michigan Avenue, Chicago, 1, Illinois. 84 pages. Revised 1964.
General analysis, plus considerable detailed information on what is being done in the different States of the U.S.A. (116/69)

Periodicals

101. *Traffic Digest & Review.*
Monthly, published by The Traffic Institute, Northwestern University, 1804, Hinman Avenue, Evanston, Illinois, U.S.A. $7 per annum. (116/73).

102. *Current Literature in Traffic and Transportation.*
Fortnightly. Published by the Traffic Institute, Northwestern University, 1804, Hinman Avenue, Evanston, Illinois, U.S.A. $5 per annum. (100/104).

103. *Highway Times.*
Roads Campaign Council, 83, Pall Mall, London, S.W.1. (116/31).

104. *Traffic Engineering & Control.*
Monthly. Printerhall Ltd., 34–40, Ludgate Hill,

London, E.C.4. £2 2s. per annum in U.K. $7 U.S.A., Canada. £2 10s. elsewhere.

105. *Fonds d'Étude et de Rechèrches sur la Sécurité Routière.*
Quarterly. 101, Rue Royale, Brussels, 1.

106. *International Road Safety & Traffic Review.*
The World Touring & Automobile Organization (O.T.A.), 32, Chesham Place, London, S.W.1.
14s. per annum.
Published quarterly in French and English. The O.T.A. provides the link between over 100 national touring, motoring and cycling organizations. It organizes an International Road Safety Congress each year. (116/45).

107. *Sécurité Routière.*
26, Rue d'Enghien, Paris (10e) France.
Bi-monthly magazine. (116/49).

108. *La Prévention Routière dans l'Entrepris.*
22, Rue du Pont-Neuf, Paris (1e).
Bi-monthly magazine. (116/50).

109. *Route et Sécurité.*
153, Avenue Jean-Jaures, Paris (19e), France.
Monthly. 1 franc. (116/51).

110.
Journals of many motorists' organization. For example *New York Motorist*, the official publication of the Automobile Club of New York; *The Open Road*, official publication of the National Road and Motorists Association (N.S.W.).
These devote considerable space to safety aspects. (116/132).

111. *Report.*
Journal of Australian Road Safety Council, 497 Collins Street, Melbourne. (116/60).

112. *Road Safety.*
Journal of Road Safety Council of N.S.W., Sydney.

Teaching

201. *Roadcraft.* (The Police Drivers' Manual.)
H.M. Stationery Office, Kingsway, London, W.C.2.
3s. 6d. 77 pages. 1960.
This appears to be intended for lay drivers, according to the introduction, as well as for Police. (116/36)

202. *Turn to Better Driving.*
Royal Society for the Prevention of Accidents, Terminal House, 52, Grosvenor Gardens, London, S.W.1.
1s. 24 pages.
Over three million copies of this have been sold. (116/37, 116/76).

203. *The Highway Code 1964.*
H.M. Stationery Office, Kingsway, London, W.C.2.
6d. 34 pages.
This is the official guide for U.K. Gives advice and also quotes the law, with references to the relevant Acts of Parliament. (116/38)

204. *Look Out Code – The Junior Road Safety Book.*
Rospa as Bib. 202. 14 pages.
Coloured pictures and simple rules covering kerb drill, etc., for young children. Many such are produced by the different road safety organizations. (116/39).

205. *Guide to the Rospa Training Centre in Road Safety.*
Rospa as Bib. 202. 1s. 48 pages.
This training centre has simple and elaborate driving simulators, driver testing devices, demonstration machines, etc. There is also a series of what might be called 'Propaganda machines' designed to illustrate key points in road tactics and perhaps to demonstrate to the

viewer that he has not absorbed some of these points as fully as he thinks he has. Some of these machines can be bought. There seems a strong case for setting up such machines in all schools, perhaps on a 'travelling circus' basis. Bored retired gentlemen with a little spare cash could have a lot of fun.

The booklet is only supplementary to a visit, not readily useable by itself. (116/40)

206. *Good Riding.*
    Rospa as Bib. 202. 1s. 24 pages.
    Prepared by Rospa with co-operation of many other motor-cycling authorities (listed on page 1). Summarizes what should be taught to young motor-cyclists. Used in R.A.C./A.C.U. scheme, 210. (116/41)

207. *Are you Good at Cycling.*
    Rospa as Bib. 202. 1s. 3d. 35 pages.
    Summarizes Rospa's views on what should be taught to young cyclists. Used in nation-wide cyclist training scheme, 209. (116/42)

208. Malfetti and Anderson.
    Critical Incidents in Behind-the-Wheel Instruction in Driver Education.
    Bulletin 330 (1962) Highway Research Board, Washington, D.C. Part of a study of driving instructors. References include:
        (9) Flanagan, J. C. 'The Critical Incident Technique.'
        Psychological Bulletin 54.4. (July 1954).
        (2) American Automobile Association 'Driver Education Reduces Accidents & Violations'.
        Washington D.C. January 1959.
    The study covers high school teachers, college instructors and high school students. The objective of the

study is to 'aid in the supervision and improvement of behind-the-wheel instruction.' For outcome see 215. (116/35)

209. National Cycling Proficiency Scheme.
Group of booklets and pamphlets, posters, badges, banners, seals, signs, pennants, etc., obtainable from Rospa (202) at very low prices. Part of wide-spread project for teaching child cyclists. Includes guide for instructors.
Reference NCP/11. 1s. 3d.

210. R.A.C./A.C.U. Training Scheme for Motor-cyclists.
Operated by Local Authorities and by motor-cycle clubs affiliated to the Auto-Cycle Union of G.B. Inaugurated by Royal Automobile Club in 1947 'to enable novices to learn to ride motor-cycles and scooters off the road'. A small fee is charged. Full facilities, including machines and training grounds are provided. Proficiency certificate is granted by independent examination at the end of the course.
Further information from R.A.C., 83, Pall Mall, London, S.W.1.

211. *The Sin that Costs Lives.*
Christian Action, 2, Amen Court, London, E.C.4.
Pamphlet giving general data, in connection with a Church Conference held January, 1955. NE1B.

212. Honolulu Traffic Code.
Tongg Publishing Company Ltd., Honolulu, Hawaii.
Covers the field in great detail. Well indexed. Based on the U.S.A. Uniform Code, 605. (116/46)

213. Australian Road Safety Council.
Annual Report 1960.
Mitchell Library, Sydney. Ref: Q 656. 1806

2

214. Florio and Stafford.
    Safety Education.
    McGraw–Hill, 1962. Mitchell Library ref: $\frac{614.8}{3}$

    Study of teaching young people. See page 210 for
    data on accidents and arrests versus trained and untrained.

215. Anderson & Malfetti.
    The Effectiveness of Teacher Performance in Behind-
    the-Wheel Instruction in Driver Education.
    Safety Research Project, Teachers College, Columbia
    University, New York. 1963.
    The outcome of Bib. 208. A specific technique for
    grading teachers. (116 /52)

216. *Man and the Motor Car.*
    The Center of Safety Education, New York University.
    Prentice-Hall, Inc., Englewood Cliffs, N.J. 6th ed. 1959.
    352 pages.
    This manual for schools was first published in 1936.
    Each chapter ends with a summary, a list of suggested
    discussion topics, a list of projects and problems, and a
    bibliography. The work was made possible financially by
    the Association of Casualty and Surety Companies.
    A separate booklet, 53 pages, *Teachers Manual for Man
    and the Motor Car* is available, giving guidance on using
    the main book.
    Separate Test Sheets for examining trainees are also
    available. (116 /65).

217. *Road Safety. A Manual for Teachers.*
    Australian Road Safety Council, Commonwealth
    Department of Shipping and Transport. Second edition
    1960. 98 pages.

218. Elkow, Heath, Seals, Smith and Stack.
    Driver Education. A student's Manual and Workbook.
    Prepared by The Center for Safety Education, New

York University, Prentice-Hall Inc., Englewood Cliffs, N.J. 164 pages. (116 /86)

219. Paterson.
Road Safety. A Manual for Teachers.
Australian Road Safety Council, Commonwealth Dept. of Shipping and Transport, Melbourne. 98 pages. 1960. (116 /57)

220. McFarland and Moore.
Youth and the Automobile.
Part of *Values and Ideals of American Youth* edited by Eli Ginzberg. Columbia University Press. 1961.
An exploratory analysis, with the general conclusion that much more factual information is needed before much can be said on this subject with certainty. (116 /9H)

221. *T.V. Programme: National Driver's Test.*
C.B.S., The Shell Oil Co., and the National Safety Council. Reported, with reproduction of viewer's test form, *Los Angeles Times*, August 30th, 1965.

222. Barmack and Payne.
The Lackland Accident Counter Measure Experiment. Highway Research Board Proceedings, Vol. 40., 1961, pages 513-522.
A controlled attempt to change attitude, in this case towards drinking. Sensational yield, but difficult to assess how much the result of intimidation, or of heightened awareness, rather than any basic change of attitude. See also Barmack and Payne, Journal of Psychology, 1961, 52, 3-24 (116 /82).

223. Coppin, Ferdun and Peck.
The Teen-aged Driver. Feb. 1965.
Publisher; as 405.
'The authors can find no evidence that, on *a statewide basis*, behind-the-wheel driver training is effective in reducing the frequency of accidents'. This does not damn

any training scheme. For example, there may be good schemes which are not sufficiently widely applied to influence the statewide results. (116/9H)

224. *Special State Financial Support for Driver Education.*
Published by the National Commission on Safety Education, National Education Association, 1201 16th Street, N.Y., Washington 6, D.C. 18 pages. 1963.
Gives a summary of State financial support in U.S.A. for Driver Education, with the source of funds and the amount made available. (116/66)

225. McCandless
Children and Adolescents.
Holt, Rinehart and Winston, New York, 1963. Lib. of Congress Cat. card no. 61-9360; 25535-0111.
Chapter 6 gives a most significant analysis of change in attitudes (largely change in self-concept) relating the magnitude of the change to the social pressure and to the real life consequences. (N.S. 136.7)

226. *Driver's Manual. New York State.*
Dept. of Motor Vehicles, 504 Central Ave., Albany 1. 48 pages. (116/97)

Causes of Accidents

301. Spicer. (See 401.)

302. Willett.
Criminal on the Road.
Tavistock Publications, 11, New Fetter Lane, London, E.C. 1964. 42s. 343 pages.
Part of The International Library of Criminology, Delinquency and Deviant Social Behaviour. Published under the auspices of the Institute for the Study and Treatment of Delinquency.
Summary of this work also in London Observer, 5th May, 1963.

Willett found that violent accidents involved criminal types more frequently than random incidence would indicate. This is in line with the evidence from vulnerability measurements (see 3.2a). He also took certain offences in which contempt for the Law and for social practices was involved (such as driving while disqualified and failing to insure) and demonstrated that the offenders had also shown their contempt in other walks of life.

To deduce from this that the ordinary motorist involved in an accident has an abnormal contempt for the Law, or is some kind of criminal, is quite unsound. This step does not appear to have been taken in the book itself, but has been written into it very freely by revenge seekers and pet theorists.

The last chapter of this book, 'Conclusions', gives some interesting general remarks, based mostly on criminological techniques. Some reasons why normal propaganda fails to influence the type of person being studied are expounded very cogently. (p. 314.) (116/118)

303. Jones.
   Theory of Traffic Collisions.
   Bib. 2, page 105.
   Recognizes the unique nature of 'visual perception'. Relates probabilities to the 'point of withdrawal', which seems to be later in the sequence than the 'confrontation' used in Chapter 2. Regarding exhortations and legal penalties, says page 108, 'improvements in skilled activities can sometimes be obtained by training before the events take place, or by making the task easier, but are most unlikely to result from a conscious attempt to try harder during the skilled activity itself'.

304. Gibbens.
   The Problem of the Young Driver.
   Bib. 2, page 99.
   Refers to experiments at Hamburg on the deterrent effect of a campaign of severity against offending motorists. Result ineffective. Gives an account of several other studies relating bad drivers and criminal offenders.

Ends 'such studies do not yet help much in preventing or curing the problem driver'. Refers to:

(a) Gibbens 'Car Thieves' British Journal of Delinquency VIII, pages 257–65.

(b) Canty 'Problem Drivers and Criminal Offenders – a Comparison.' Canadian Services Medical Journal XII, 136–43.

(c) Lewrentz 1960. Kriminal Biologische Gegenwartsfragen 4.66. 21–32 Stuttgart.

305. Eysenck.
   The Driver – His Mind.
   Bib. 2, page 1.
   Refers to involuntary rest pauses (in effect blackouts of attention), the frequency of which increases with monotony and tiredness, and also when alcohol has been taken. This suggests a limit to the observation of vulnerabilities when tired.

306. Moseley.
   Harvard University.
   Moseley was Head of a Harvard University Team conducting a five-year programme of research into fatal highway collisions. London *Times*, 7th January, 1963, reporting the halfway progress, quoting from a Bulletin of the Fédération Internationale de l'Automobile, says: 'Doctor Moseley rejects official safety slogans, such as "Slow down and live" ... contending that if the problems and their solutions were as simple as this, the road death rate should be negligible ... "If chance is the dominant factor," he says, "the problem is not subject to control." '
   Moseley thinks that the collision deaths case is related to damage and injury cases only to some limited extent – the differences are greater than the similarities. (116/109)

307. Turton.
   Head of Road Traffic Department of Bedfordshire Police.

Reported in London *Times*, 8th January, 1965, as saying that nine out of every ten accidents on the M1 Motorway were caused by drivers falling asleep. 'I would advise drivers to try and keep changing the tone of the engine noise, drive with a window open, and not to drive too far at a stretch.' (116/103)

308. Eysenck.
Fact and Fiction in Psychology, Penguin Book A696.
Chapter 6, 'Accidents and Personality' discusses chiefly road accidents. There may be, as in 302, a tendency to overestimate the importance of the abnormal.

309. Tanner.
Reduction of Accidents by Improved Street Lighting.
Light and Lighting 1958, 51(11).

310. Goldstein.
The Public Health Service Research Grants Program in Accident Prevention.
Research Grants Branch Division of Accident Prevention, Public Health Service, Washington 25, D.C.
Adapted from a presentation at the Seventh Stapp Automotive Crash Conference, November 13, 1963, Los Angeles.
References to the publications derived from this program are contained in another brochure (27 pages) also compiled by Dr. Goldstein, and available from the same source as above. (116/94)

311. Haddon, Suchman, and Klein.
Accident Research: Methods and Approaches.
Harper and Row, New York and London. 752 pages. 1964.

312. Haddon.
Alcohol and Highway Accidents.
Proceedings of the Third International Conference on Alcohol and Road Traffic, London. September 1962.

British Medical Association, Tavistock Square, London, W.C.I. (116/88).

313. Birrell.
Alcohol as a Factor in Victorian Road Collisions.
Medical Journal of Australia, May 7, 1960. (116/9)

314. Adams.
The Association Between Smoking and Accidents.
Address before the Safety Convention and Exposition of the Greater New York Safety Council, New York City, April 6, 1964. (116/92)

315. *What Motorists really Think about Traffic Safety.*
A.T.A. Foundation, Inc. 1424 16th Street, N.W., Washington 6, D.C. or the Pure Oil Co. Booklet. 16 pages.
Study by the Opinion Research Corporation aimed at determining whether mass communications can motivate people to become safe drivers and if so, what approaches would be most effective. (116/70)

Driver Characteristics

401. Spicer.
Human Factors in Traffic Accidents, May 1964.
Department of Health, Honolulu.
Covers a three year investigation sponsored by U.S. Public Health Service* endeavouring to identify the driver characteristics or patterns that cause accidents. Four characteristics were investigated – level of self-appraisal, visual perception, aggressive tendencies, problem-solving ability.
Conclusions reached: 'Visual perception appears to be a critical factor in driving behaviour. As a learned skill it is probably amenable to teaching methods.'
A quotation from this report is given in 3·4.
This report includes a comprehensive summary of the research position with bibliography, including:

*Supported by U.S. Public Health Service Grant No. AC–55 from the Mental Health Division, Hawaii Department of Health.

   (i) McFarland Moore and Warren – Human Variables in motor-vehicle Accidents – a review of the Literature. Boston, Harvard School of Public Health, 1955.

  (ii) Shaw – Objective Measurement of Driving Skill. Traffic Safety Research Review, December 1958, 2 (4). 13–16.

 (iii) Brody, L. Accidents and Attitudes. Psychology of Safety. Centre for Safety Education, New York University, 1959. (116/32)

402. Malfetti.
Traffic Safety, the Driver and Electronics.
Teachers' College Record, Vol. 61, No. 2, November 1959.

An analysis of the basic situation, much closely relevant to the present study. For example: 'The significant personal characteristics seem to be so highly personal that it is uneconomical at best, and perhaps hopeless, to do anything about them for the limited purpose of improving driver behaviour.'
Contains valuable bibliography including:

   (6) Häkkinen Sauli.
Traffic Accidents and Driver Characteristics. Helsinki, Finland. Institute of Technology Scientific Researches No. 13, 1958. 198 pages.

   (9) Jones.
Planning for intensive investigation of Behavioral Aspects of Traffic Accidents. Evanston, Illinois.
Traffic Institute, North-western University, 1958. 81 pages.

  (18) Malfetti.
Electronic Techniques for Traffic Control and Safety.
State Government, 31: 240–44, Autumn 1958. (116/34)

403. Eysenck. Bib. 305.

404. Somerville.
   The Driver – His Health – Cardiac.
   Bib. 2, page 12.
   Indicates that sudden collapse from heart attack is not a negligible factor. (Deaths greater than 1 per 22,000 driver years = equivalent to 8% of all deaths.) Regarding medical tests on drivers, refers, *inter alia*, to:

   (1) Journal of American Medical Association 169.1195, 1959.
   (2) British Medical Association, 1954.
       Memorandum on medical standards for road, rail and air transport.
   (3) World Health Organization, 1956.
       Guiding Principles in Medical Examination for driving Permits.

405. *The 1964 Californian Driver Record Study.*
   State of California. Dept. of Motor Vehicles. Division of Adminstration Research and Statistics Section.
   Part 1. Introduction and Methodological Description.
   Part 2. Accidents, Traffic Citations and Negligent Operator Count by Sex.
       Too many factors, such as period of day when women do most of their driving, make most conclusions far from certain.

406. Goldstein.
   Human Variables in Traffic Accidents.
   Division of Engineering and Industrial Research, National Academy of Sciences – National Research Council. 8 pages.
   An invaluable summary of the position with indications of the significance of different research, and a selected Bibliography of 54 items. Says, page 2, 'It also appears that it is not the few with deviant behaviour which account for the major proportion of the problem, but the extremely many who behave in ways that are condoned'.
   This conclusion appears to be derived partly from the 6-year Connecticut Study published in 1938. It is interesting that apparently the same experiment was

used by the authors of *Man and the Motor Car* (Bib. 216) to justify precisely the opposite conclusion. They say, page 125, 6th edition 'A large percentage of our accidents is caused by a small percentage of drivers'.

Presumably this Connecticut Study is item 51 of the Goldstein paper:

U.S. Congress. 'Motor Vehicle Traffic Conditions in the United States, the Accident Prone Driver'. House Document No. 462, part vi, Washington D.C. Government Printing Office 1938.

An analysis of these Connecticut results is referred to in item 20 of the Goldstein paper:

Forbes. The Normal Automobile Driver as a Traffic Problem. Journal of General Psychology No. 20, pp. 471, 474 (1939).

Dr. Goldstein was good enough to give me the following comments:

It is true that in any one period only a small proportion of all drivers are involved in accidents. In Washington, D.C., this is approximately 5% per year – we might say that 5% caused *all* the accidents in a given year. But in a *subsequent* year it is an almost *entirely different* 5% who are involved in the accidents! In the Connecticut study 76% of the accident *repeaters* of the first triennium were accident-free in the second triennium. Of those who had *one* accident in the first period 83% were accident-free in the second. Of those who were accident-free in the first, 91% were accident-free in the second. Those drivers who were accident-free in the first period (89% of the total group studied) accounted for 79% of all accidents in the second period. I hope this clarifies the point. (116/63)

407. Goldstein.
Research on Human Variables in Safe Motor Vehicle Operation.
The Driver Behaviour Research Project, The George Washington University, Washington, D.C.
Reprinted by U.S. Dept. of Health, Education and Welfare, Division of Accident Prevention, Washington, D.C., 20201. 1964. 42 pages.

A tabular summary of many of the best known research projects in this field, with critical comments. Including estimates of validity (significance) (116/93).

408. McFarland and Moseley.
   Human Factors in Highway Transport Safety.
   Harvard School of Public Health, 695 Huntingdon Avenue, Boston. 1954.
   This is a voluminous report, covering a wide range, and a rich source of data. It is the only study where I have found the 'vulnerability' concept used. In a study of truck driver 'errors' – clearly very close to vulnerabilities – a pattern was discerned. The actual results appear to contradict those reported in 4.3, regarding tiredness. (116/9H)

409. Barmack and Others.
   Driver Personality and Behaviour Characteristics.
   Highway Research Board Bulletin 285.
   National Academy of Sciences – National Research Council. Publication 855.
   Includes a balanced assessment of the role of alcohol, with valuable bibliography, and suggestions for further research. (116/83)

410. McFarland, Tune and Welford.
   On the Driving of Automobiles by Older People.
   Journal of Gerontology, Vol. 19, No. 2. April 1964.
   Indicates (1) that the older group clearly has a worse accident record than average; (2) that slowness occurs in all kinds of responses in old age (may be aggravated by complexity of choice, and masked by other factors); (3) the incidence and progress of deterioration varied so widely from individual to individual that any general rule is unreachable.
   This paper refers to a deterioration in *short term* memory, which could well lead to a fruitful line of research. Gives valuable list of references. (116/9H)

411. Coppin & Peck.
   The Totally Deaf Driver in California.

Publisher as 405. Part 1 1963. Part 2 1964.
Indicates decided danger from deaf males. This must surely also imply a danger from loud radio in cars.

412. *The Danger Hour.*
Autogineer, February 1965. Staff Magazine General Motors Technical Centre, Warren, Michigan.
Suggests that we are twice as dangerous as drivers on the way home as we are on the way to work. (116/64.)

413. Berkowitz, editor.
Advances in Experimental Social Psychology, Vol. 1.
Academic Press, 111 5th Avenue, N.Y., N.Y. 10003.
319 pages. $9.00
See especially section by Walters and Parke on Social Motivation.

414. See Bib. 1. Sub references cited.

Pedestrians

501. Garwood and Moore (Road Research Lab. U.K.).
Pedestrian Accidents.
Bib. 2, page 89.
General survey of pedestrian accidents and some methods of reduction. Cites one investigation where pedestrian risks are reduced by Zebra crossings, as compared with short-cut crossings, to a quarter; by traffic control lights to one-twentythird.
Most pedestrians are hit crossing the roads. These accidents are so concentrated geographically that there is an opportunity for a radical solution, such as complete segregation of vehicles and pedestrians. (Compare the Radburn experiment and U.K. derivatives.)

502. Haddon, Valien, McCarroll and Umberger.
A Controlled Investigation of the Characteristics of Adult Pedestrians Fatally Injured by Motor Vehicles in Manhattan.

Journal of Chronic Diseases, St. Louis. Vol. 14, No. 6., pp. 655-678. December 1961. (116/90)

The Police and the Law

601. Police Drivers' Manual. (See Bib. 201.)

602. Highway Code, G.B. (See Bib. 203.)
   Highway Code, Honolulu. (See Bib. 212.)
   Drivers Manual: N.Y. State. (See Bib. 226.)

603. Gott. (Chief Constable of Northamptonshire).
   Prosecution Warning or Advice?
   Bib. 2, page 29.
   Gives an account of some attempts to improve traffic accident figures by appeals and warnings, with generally disappointing results. Bib. 11 records better results obtained by such methods.

604. Walker. (Chief Constable, Eastbourne).
   The Orthodox is not necessarily the Answer.
   Bib. 2, page 33.
   Describes success of experiment giving priority at crossroads by white lines across the subsidiary road. Claims 66% reduction of casualties.

605. *Uniform Vehicle Code. Model Traffic Ordinance. Traffic Laws Annual.* National Committee on Uniform Traffic Laws & Ordinances. 1319 18th Street, N.W., Washington, D.C., 20036. (100/111)

606. Blom-Cooper.
   Murder and the Motor Car.
   London, *Sunday Times*, 12th January, 1964.
   Refers to case of Gypsy Jim Smith who in 1960 killed a policeman demonstrably without intending to, and was judged guilty of murder. Court of Criminal Appeal substituted manslaughter. House of Lords restored original verdict of capital murder, carrying the death

sentence. The article studies the basic ethics involved, and refers to Barbara Wootton and others who consider that there is over-emphasis on intent and that effects should be considered in determining penalties. (116/11)

607. Blom-Cooper and Morris.
A Calendar of Murder.
Michael Joseph Limited. (116/11)

608. Muffett.
Letter to London *Times* on Compensation for Accidents, 22nd February, 1965.
Says opinion is developing in legal circles in favour of a comprehensive insurance scheme such that negligence is no longer the determining factor. Cf. 612. (As things stand today, if you kill me by accident my wife may do very well out of it. If you do it deliberately, she may well starve.) (116/12)

609. Hayek.
The Road to Serfdom.
Dymocks Book Arcade, Sydney. 1944.
Published also in London.

610. Coppin, Marsh and Peck.
A Re-evaluation of Group Driver Improvement Meetings.
Publisher as 405.
Gives suggested material for such meetings. About 15 people per meeting. Records of 1,440 meeting group participants and 610 controls were examined. P.43 has excellent summary of all aspects.
The conclusions are that the Driver Improvement Meeting programme does not appear to reduce accidents, but does improve convictions. There is no apparent difference between receiving a notice and attending a meeting. It would seem justifiable to conclude that exhortations have failed and that intimidation has misfired towards avoiding the police, instead of safety. (116/9H)

611. Coppin and van Oldenbeek.
Driving Under Suspension and Revocation.
Report No. 18. Jan. 1965.
Publisher as 405.

The Department has issued 86,000 suspensions and 36,000 revocation orders.

The results are a wonderful example of the flouting of the law that can be induced, and of the limits to intimidation. 36 out of every 100 suspended, and 68 out of every 100 revoked-negligent, drivers drove during suspension or revocation. The reality is probably even worse, because many would be very canny in not being caught. (116 /9H)

612. *Third Commonwealth and Empire Law Conference, Sydney, Australia.* August, 1965.
Sweet & Maxwell, Ltd., London, The Law Book Co. Ltd., Australia.

Several papers presented at this Conference, considering the fundamentals of the legal position, are of considerable value:

Herron and Asprey give a summary of the lines of thought being followed in many different countries together with a suggestion for discussion regarding the handling of compensation cases.

Richardson considers the basic legal structure, and emphasizes that the vast majority of motoring cases involve what may properly be called a misjudgement and should be treated as civil offences and not criminal offences.

Napley also gives a general analysis and includes one particularly interesting suggestion – the use of a postponed disqualification.

McRuer explores the basic philosophy as well as the legal problems, and presents a formidable picture of the extreme difficulty both in framing and in administering the law.

613. Hardie & McCallum.
Medico-legal aspects of the road toll and breath alcohol analysis as an aid to law enforcement.

Proceedings of the Medico-legal Society of New South Wales 1963-1964. (116/96)

Statistics

701. *Statistics of Road Traffic Accidents in Europe 1960.*
United Nations, Palais des Nations, Geneva, June 1962. 3s. 6d.
UNO Reference: E/ECE/465.
E/ECE/TKAWS/528.
Very good set of data.

702. Goodhart
Statistics.
Bib. 2, page 17.
Gives illustrations of dangers in interpreting statistics.

703. Fisher.
The Design of Experiments.
This is apparently regarded as the standard work on the significance of figures as they appear in statistics.
'Significance' is a technical term in this connection.

704. Loveday.
A First Course in Statistics. 122 pages.
A Second Course in Statistics. 156 pages.
Cambridge University Press, 1964.
These two small books are a splendid point of entry, and give enough information for an understanding of most sociological investigations.

705. Chambers.
Statistical Calculation for Beginners.
Cambridge University Press, 1964. 168 pages.
A particularly valuable book for those who would like to make use of the methods, without worrying too much about the underlying mathematics.

706. von Mises.
Mathematical Theory of Probability and Statistics.

Edited and complemented by Hilda Geiringer.
Academic Press, 111 5th Avenue, New York, N.Y. 10003
Berkeley Square House, London, W.1. 1964. 694 pages.
(116/134)

707. Mr. A. E. O'dell's list:–
Statistical Mathematics. A. C. Aitken 1957. Oliver & Boyd.
Statistics and their Application to Commerce. 1956. A. L.
Boddington. HFL.
Introduction to Statistics for the Social Sciences. T. G. Conolly
and anr. 1957. Cleaver-Hume Press.
Statistics in Theory and Practice. J. R. Connor. 1957.
Pitmans.
Statistical Methods in Research and Production. O. L. Davies
for I.C.I. Oliver & Boyd.
Statistical Methods and Scientific Inference. Sir R. A. Fisher.
1956. Oliver & Boyd.
Statistical Theory. L. T. Hogben. 1957. G. Allen & Unwin.
Advanced Theory of Statistics. M. G. Kendall. 1958. Ch.
Griffin and other works.
Combination of Observations. W. M. Smart. 1958. Cambridge
U.P.
Business Statistics & Statistical Method. G. L. Thirkettle.
1957. Macdonald & Evans.
Statistical Methods in Biology. N. T. J. Bailey. 1959. English
U.P.
Use and Abuse of Statistics. W. T. Reichman. 1961. Methuen
Uses of Economic Statistics. C. A. Blyth. 1960. Allen &
Unwin.
Modern Elementary Statistics. J. F. Freund. 1960. Prentice-
Hall.
Elements of Statistics. E. B. Mode. 1961. Prentice-Hall.
First Course in Mathematical Statistics. C. E. Weatherburn.
1961. Cambridge U.P. (NEI.O)

Index

B1(32) refers to Bibliography Item 1 Subcitation (32)
n.r. signifies that this aspect had not been referred to.

Teaching—*contd.*
  by thinking, 95
  can create closed mind, 75, 99
  car out of control, 94
  crossing road, 117
  dangers of, 98–100
  discipline, 84–88
  employees, 152
  handling car, 92, 188
  limitations of, 152, 189
  mathematics, 75, 195
  mechanics of car, 92
  morality, 88–89, 186
  no panacea, 152
  observation of vulnerabilities, 96
  Police School, Hendon, B201
  Rospa view on material, B202
  skidding, 93
  special groups, 91
  textbooks, B200
  the alchemist, 167
  the right time, 98
  traffic tactics, 90
  two-stage processes, 92, 188
  visual perception, 66, 96–98
  uncertainty as to results, 92
  see also education, instructors
technical literature, unreliable, 182
tests, see driving tests
theft of cars, n.r.
Thesinger, Mr Justice, 184
thinking, 14, 69, 95, 169
  necessity for, 13, 70, 167
  refusal to, 68, 69, 167
  stimulated by observing vulnerabilities, 96
  v. learning by rote, 95
threat of collision, 30, 44
tickets, see citations
tiredness, 53, 114, B305, B307
tires, B26
tolerance, limits to, 88
toughness, see getting tough
Traffic Institute, Evanston, 101, 102, B4
traffic lights, n.r.
traffic tactics, 90, 198, 202
trailers, n.r.
trucks, bad condition, 118
two-stage learning, 92, 188
tyres, B26

unawareness of danger, 37, 115
unions, trade, 86, 127

values, sense of, 120
violations,
  compared to burglary, 131, 133
  do they cause accidents?, 129
  flagrant, 132
  frequency of, 130
  per citation, 130
  plain clothes patrols, 138
  related to vulnerabilities, 131
  thousands per annum, 130
  unbooked, 138, 195
violent accidents, 37, 50, 115, 183, B306
visual acuity, 28
visual perception, 28, 97, B401
  acquiring from experience, 29, 97
  teaching of, 66, 96–98
vulnerability, 29, 193
  as threat, 30, 44
  booklet on, 44–50
  common standards, 29, 30
  counting, 29, 46, 47, 50, 55
  determined by driver's judgment, 96
  examples of, 198–202
  experiment on, 43, 51–58
  100 x normal, 37
  propaganda, yield from, 57, 58
  psychological resistance, 54
  rate, 28, 36, 38
  recognition of, 56
  related to accidents, 36, 131
  related to violations, 131
  retention of idea, 50, 56, 65, 74
  sudden reduction, 36, 133
  youths, high, 36

warning signals, in brain, 66
whiplash injury, 123
wild drivers, 37, 111, 113
  buccaneers, 112, 113
  different categories of, 112
  effect of police presence, 38
  habitual, 38, 196
  proportion of collisions, 39
  racers, 113
  youths, proportion of, 38, 39, 45, 193, 195
Willett, Dr T. C., 146, B302
witness, lying, 158, 184
women drivers, 202, B1(23), B15
wrestling, addiction to, 85

youths,
  breaking in, 84
  compared colts, 85
  corruption of, 186
  creating anxiety, 155, 194
  high proportion uncivilized, 87
  high vulnerability, 36, 112
  intimidation of, 87
  killing by, 104
  lack of visual perception, 108
  patience, need for, 88, 112, 134, 154–155, 170, 202
  persecution of, 202
  provisional licences, 154
  teaching from scratch, 94
  see also, barbarian invasion, behaviour changing, deterrents, discipline, getting tough